SpeakEasy Spanish

Survival Spanish
for
First Responders

Myelita Melton, MA

SpeakEasy Communications, Incorporated

SpeakEasy's Survival Spanish for First Responders

Author: Myelita A. Melton
Cover Design: Ellen Wass Beckerman
Published by SpeakEasy Communications, Incorporated
116 Sea Trail Drive
Mooresville, NC 28117-8493
USA

ISBN 10:   0-9712593-8-0
ISBN-13:   978-0-9712593-8-0

Survival Spanish for First Responders, SpeakEasy Spanish, SpeakEasy's Survival Spanish, SpeakEasy's Survival Spanish for First Responders, and SpeakEasySpanish.com are either trademarks or registered trademarks of SpeakEasy Communications, Inc. in the United States and/or other countries.

The content of this book is furnished for informational use only, is subject to change without notice, and should not be construed as a commitment by SpeakEasy Communications, Incorporated. SpeakEasy Communications, Incorporated assumes no responsibility or liability for any errors, omissions, or inaccuracies that may appear in the informational content contained in this guide.

Foreword

This book is dedicated to the police, firefighters and paramedics in the great cities of New York and New Orleans. Thank you for raising our awareness of the dangers you face daily and for capturing our hearts. Like first responders everywhere, you are all true heroes!

Special mention also goes to Stuart Blair for his excellent photography and to the firefighters of Clark County Fire District 10 in Amboy, Washington, especially Scott who is shown on the cover.

I'd also like to thank the fire department in Mooresville, North Carolina for giving me my first glimpse into the life of a first responder. I've never had more fun teaching!

Survival Spanish for First Responders
Table of Contents

Using This Material

Survival Spanish for First Responders from SpeakEasy Spanish™ is designed for adults with no previous experience in the Spanish language. Through research and interviews with professionals in your field, we have developed this material as a practical guide to using Spanish on the job. Wherever possible, we have chosen to use the similarities between English and Spanish to facilitate your success.

Throughout the manual, you will find study tips and pronunciation guides that will help you to say the words correctly. In the guides, we have broken down the Spanish words for you by syllable, choosing English words that closely approximate the required Spanish sound. This method makes learning Spanish more accessible because it doesn't seem as foreign. When you see letters that are **BOLD** in the guide, say that part of the word the loudest. The bold capital letters will show you where the emphasis falls for that word.

At SpeakEasy Communications, we believe that *communication* is more important than *conjugation*, and that what you learn must be practical for what you do. We urge you to set realistic, practical goals. Make practice a regular part of your day and you will be surprised at the progress you make!

Introdución to Latin America

What's The Proper Term?
Both!

Latino/Latina: Anyone from Latin America who speaks Spanish as his or her native language.

Hispanic: Anyone who speaks Spanish as his or her native language and traces family origin to Spain.

Note: Don't assume that anyone who speaks Spanish is Mexican. They could be from *anywhere* in Latin America.

Hispanics in America mainly come from the following areas:

1. **Mexico**
2. **Central and South America**
3. **Puerto Rico**
4. **Cuba**

Many Latinos from El Salvador, Honduras and Guatemala came to America because of Hurricane Mitch in 1998.

According to US Census:

1. There are over 43 million in the US who speak Spanish.
2. Hispanics are the nation's majority minority.
3. By 2050, Hispanics will make up an estimated 25% of the US population.
4. Currently ten southeastern states have the fastest growing Hispanic populations.
5. Over 17% of the nation's school-aged children are Latino.
6. In 2007, Latino buying power is expected to increase to over 900 billion dollars.
7. 47% of Hispanics in the US are limited in English proficiency.

SpeakEasy's Secrets to Learning Spanish

Congratulations on your decision to learn Spanish! This decision is one of the smartest choices you will ever make, considering the increasing diversity in our country. It's definitely one you will never regret. You are now among a growing number of America's visionary leaders who want to build more trusting relationships with Hispanic-Americans, the fastest growing segment of our population.

Learning Spanish is going to open many doors for you, and it will affect you in ways you can't imagine. By learning Spanish, you will be able to work more efficiently and safely in almost every workplace in the nation. Since bilingual employees are currently in short supply nationwide, you will find increasing job opportunities in almost every profession. In addition, you will be able to build stronger relationships with Latinos you meet everywhere you go. There's also another added benefit: You are going to raise your communication skills to a whole new level.

As an adult, learning a new language requires a certain mindset. It takes time, patience and more than a little stubbornness. Think about it. You didn't learn English overnight. You began crying as an infant. That was your first attempt at communication. Later you uttered syllables. When you did, your parents thought you were the world's smartest child, and they rewarded you constantly. After a few years, you began to form simple sentences. If you are like me, by the time you reached your first class in school, you couldn't stop talking. Therefore, you can't expect to know everything about Spanish by studying it for only a few weeks. You must give Spanish some time to sink in just as English did.

It's also important for you to realize that adults learn languages differently than children. Kids learn by listening and by imitating. For them, learning Spanish or any other second language is relatively easy because their brains learn naturally. It's part of human development. Then you reach puberty and everything changes! Your body sets your speech pattern for its native language.

For many people, this is the age when their language learning center slows down or turns completely off. Your body just figures it doesn't need it any longer. Coincidentally, this slow-down occurs about the same time that you hit your seventh grade Spanish class. That's why learning Spanish seemed to be so hard — that, and the huge amount of very impractical things you were forced to learn. As a result of this physical change in puberty, adults tend to learn languages more visually. However, listening and imitating are still important, especially when paired with a visual cue. Most adults benefit from seeing a Spanish word spelled phonetically and hearing it at the same time. This combination helps your brain make sense of the new sounds.

Adults are also practical learners. If you see a reason for what you are studying, you will find learning easier to accomplish. It is very true that if you practice your Spanish daily, you are less likely to lose it. Yes, you can teach an old dog new tricks! You are *never* too old to learn Spanish.

If you did take Spanish in high school or college, you are going to be pleasantly surprised when words and phrases you thought you had forgotten begin to come back to you. That previous experience with other languages is still in your mind. It's just hidden away in a seldom used filing cabinet. Soon that cabinet will open up again, and that will help you learn new words even faster.

Here's another thought you should consider. *What they told you in the traditional foreign language classroom is not exactly correct.* There's no such thing as *"perfect Spanish"* just as there is no *"perfect English."* This fact leaves the door for good communication wide open!

The secret to learning Spanish is having *self-confidence and a great sense of humor.* To build self-confidence, you must realize that the entire learning experience is painless and fun. Naturally, you are going to make mistakes — everyone does. We all make mistakes in English too! So get ready to laugh and learn. ***Don't think that you must have a perfect Spanish sentence in your head*** *before you say something.* It's very important for you to say what you know — even if it's only a word or two. The point is to communicate. Communication doesn't have to be "pretty" or perfect to be effective.

Español is one of the world's most precise and expressive languages. Consider these other important facts as you begin to "*habla español*":

- ✓ English and Spanish share a common Latin heritage, so literally thousands of words in our two languages are either *similar* or *identical.*

- ✓ Your ability to communicate is the most important thing, so your grammar and pronunciation don't have to be "*perfect*" for you to be understood.

- ✓ Some very practical and common expressions in Spanish can be communicated with a few simple words.

- ✓ As the number of Latinos in the United States increases, so do your opportunities to practice. Saying even a phrase or two in Spanish every day will help you learn faster.

- ✓ Relax! People who enjoy their learning experiences acquire Spanish at a much faster pace than others.

- ✓ Set realistic goals and establish reasonable practice habits.

- ✓ When you speak even a little Spanish, you are showing a tremendous respect for the Hispanic culture and its people.

- ✓ Even a little Spanish or *poco español* goes a long way!

As you begin the process of learning Spanish, you are going to notice a few important differences. Speaking Spanish is going to feel and sound a little odd to you at first. This feeling is completely normal; you are using muscles in your face that English doesn't require and your inner ear is not accustomed to hearing you speak

Spanish. People tell me it sounds and feels like a cartoon character has gotten inside your head! Don't let that stop you. Keep right on going!

Many Americans know more Spanish than they realize, and they can pronounce many words perfectly. Review the list below. How many of the Spanish words do you recognize? Using what you already know about Spanish will enable you to learn new things easier and faster — it's a great way to build your confidence.

Amigos Similares y Familiares

Americano	Amigo	Hospital	Español	Doctor
Loco	Hotel	Oficina	Agua	Fiesta
Dinero	Señor	Señorita	Señora	Sombrero
Burrito	Taco	Olé	No problema	Accidente
Nachos	Salsa	Teléfono	Quesadilla	Margarita

The Sounds of Spanish

No se preocupe. Don't worry. One of your biggest concerns about acquiring a new language will be speaking it well enough so that others can understand you. Spanish is close enough to English that making a few mistakes along the way won't hurt your ability to communicate.

The most important sounds in Spanish consist of *five* vowels. Each one is pronounced the way it is written. Spanish vowels are never *silent*. Even if there are two vowels together in a word, both of them will stand up and be heard.

A	(ah)	as in mama
E	(eh)	as in "hay or the "eh" in set
I	(ee)	as in deep
O	(oh)	as in open
U	(oo)	as in spoon

Here are the other sounds you'll need to remember. Always pronounce them the same way. Spanish is a very consistent language; the sounds the letters make don't shift around as much as they do in English.

Spanish Letter		English Sound
C	(before an e or i)	s as in Sam: **cero**: SAY-row
G	(before an e or i)	h as in he: **energía**: n-air-HE-ah
		emergencia: a-mare-HEN-see-ah
H		silent: **hacienda**: ah-see-N-da
J		h as in hot: **Julio**, HOO-lee-oh
LL		y as in yoyo: **tortilla**, tor-TEE-ya
Ñ		ny as in canyon: **español**, es-pan-NYOL
QU		k as in kit: **tequila**, tay-KEY-la
RR		Trilled r sound: **burro**, BOO-row
V		v as in Victor: **Victor**, Vic-TOR
Z		s as in son: **Gonzales**, gone-SA-les

**Note: People from Latin American countries have a variety of accents just like Americans. In certain areas of Latin America, people tend to pronounce the letter "v" more like the English letter "b." This tendency is particularly true in parts of Mexico. In other Latin American countries, a "v" sounds like an English "v." If you learned to switch the "v" sound for a "b" sound in high school or college Spanish classes, don't change your habit; however, if you have had no experience with Spanish before now, don't sweat the small stuff! Pronounce the "v" as you normally would.

The Other Consonants: The remaining letters in Spanish have very similar sounds to their equivalent in English.

The Spanish Alphabet
El alphabeto español

A	ah	J	HO-ta	R	AIR-ray
B	bay	K	ka	RR	EH-rray
C	say	L	L-ay	S	S-ay
CH	chay	LL	A-yea	T	tay
D	day	M	M-ay	U	oo
E	A or EH	N	N-ay	V	vay
F	f-ay	Ñ	N-yea	W	DOE-blay-vay
G	hay	O	oh	X	A-kees
H	AH-chay	P	pay	Y	ee-gree-A-gah
I	ee	Q	coo	Z	SAY-ta

Did you notice something different about the Spanish alphabet? It has four letters the English alphabet doesn't have. Can you find them?

The Four "Extra" Letters

Look carefully at the table above which contains the Spanish alphabet. Did you notice that the Spanish language contains more letters in its alphabet than English? There are thirty letters in the Spanish alphabet. Even though Spanish has more letters in its alphabet, none of them will present *problemas* for you. Here are the four extra letters and words in which they are used:

CH   Sounds like the following English words: Chuck, Charlie and Chocolate. Try saying these Spanish words: Nacho and macho

LL   Sounds essentially like an English "y." However, you will hear slight variations depending on where the person who is speaking Spanish to you is originally from. **Example**: Tortilla (tor-T-ya)

7

Ñ   Sounds like a combination of "ny" as in canyon or onion:
      Example: español (es-pan-**NYOL**)

RR   This letter is a "trilled" sound. Practice by taking your tongue and placing it on the roof of your mouth just behind your front teeth. Now blow air across the tip of your tongue and make it flutter. This sound can be difficult for some adults to make. It's only strange because you are moving your tongue muscle in a new way. Since there are no words in English with trilled sounds, you just never learned to move your tongue that way. Children learning Spanish have no trouble at all with this sound. Like any new activity, it will take time, patience and practice! Don't let a problem with the trilled "r" stop you from speaking. Essentially the sounds of the English "r" and the Spanish "r" are the same. To start, say the double "r" a bit louder than a single "r."

      Example: Burrito (boo-**REE**-toe)

The Spanish Accent

In Spanish, you will see two types of accent marks. Both marks are very important and do different things. One of the marks you will notice is called a "tilde." It is only found over the letter "N." But, don't get the Ñ confused with N. The accent mark over Ñ turns it into a different letter entirely. In fact, it's one of four letters in the Spanish alphabet that the English alphabet doesn't have. The Ñ changes the sound of the letter to a combination of "ny." You'll hear the sound that this important letter makes in the English words "canyon" and "onion."

Occasionally you will see another accent mark over a letter in a Spanish word. The accent mark or "slash" mark shows you where to place vocal emphasis. So, when you see an accent mark over a letter in a Spanish word, just say that part of the word louder. For example: José (ho-**SAY**). These accented syllables are indicated in our pronunciation guides with bold, capital letters.

Pronouncing Spanish Words

The pronunciation of Spanish words follows very basic, consistent rules. This regular pattern makes the language easier to learn. Here are some tips to remember:

1. Most Spanish words that end with a vowel are stressed or emphasized on the *next to the last* syllable.
   Señorita: sen-your-**REE**-ta   Jalapeño: ha-la-**PAIN**-yo

2. Look for an accent mark. If the Spanish word has an accent in it, that's the emphasized syllable.
   José: ho-**SAY**   ¿Cómo está?: **KO**-mo es-**TA**

3. Words that end in consonants are stressed on the *final* syllable.
   Doctor: doc-**TOR**   Hotel: oh-**TELL**

Spanish Punctuation Marks

Spanish has two different punctuation marks than English does. Both of them are upside down versions of English punctuation marks. They are used to signal you that something other than a simple declarative sentence is just ahead.

First, there's the upside down question mark (¿). You will see it at the beginning of all questions. It's there simply to let you know that what follows is a question and you will need to give your voice an upward inflection. It's the same inflection we use in English.

Example: Do you speak English?   ¿Habla inglés?

Second, there's the upside down exclamation mark (¡). It lets you know that what follows should be vocally emphasized.

Example: Hi!   ¡Hola!

Spanglish

Much of the southwestern part of the United States originally belonged to Mexico. In 1848, after the US-Mexican War, the border was moved south to the Rio Grande River. The treaty that was signed at the end of the conflict transformed Spanish-speaking Mexicans into Americans overnight! Imagine waking up one morning and finding out that you are a citizen of another country, and that you have to learn a new language! As a result, an entirely new slang language was born that mixes the best of both worlds — *Spanglish*.

In America, Spanglish really started to come into its own in the early 1970s. At that time, it gained popularity and the number of vocabulary words increased. Now, people who use Spanglish span generations, classes and nationalities. It's heard in pop music, seen in print, and used in conversations throughout Latin America. It isn't just an American phenomenon. Immigrants may turn to Spanglish out of necessity while they are learning English, and bilingual speakers use it because it's convenient. If you listen to native speakers carefully, you will hear them use a mixture of languages. Sometimes in the middle of a conversation, you may hear an English word or two. People who speak Spanish tend to use whatever word or phrase suits their purpose and is most descriptive. In general conversation, it doesn't matter what language it is. Even though Spanglish is still frowned upon in most traditional language classes and by those who want to keep the Spanish language "pure," it really is a great tool for most people.

Common Spanglish Words

Truck/Trocka	Lunch/Lonche	No parking/No parque
Yard/Yarda	Break/Breaka	Cell phone/Cel
Carpet/Carpeta	Check/Chequear	Market/Marketa
Push/Puchar	Roof/Ruffo	Email/Email

Amigos Familiares

Using what you have learned about how Spanish sounds, practice the words listed below. Examine them carefully. Each word bears a strong resemblance to its English counterpart, or it's a common Spanish word used by many people who don't speak Spanish. Begin by carefully and slowly pronouncing each word on the list. If you are having trouble, go back and review the vowel sounds again. Continue by reviewing the section on Spanish accents and pronunciation. Reviewing these three concepts will be helpful as you continue building your skills. Practice these similar and familiar words often. They will help you remember the basic, important sounds of *español*.

Accidente	Desorden público	Incendio
Agresión	Divorcio	Infracción
Alarma	Doctor	Interrogación
Alcohol	Documento	Legal
Alerta máxima	Escandalosa	Medicina
Ambulancia	Estómago	Médico
Argumentativo	Explique	Menor
Arma	Factores	Paciente
Arresto	Familia	Perpetrador *un criminal*
Asalto	Fractura	Petición
Ataque	Fuego	Policía
Bebé	Gasolina	Progreso
Bomba *- Pump*	Grave	Pulmones
Cárcel *- Jail*	Historia penal *criminal record*	Químicos
Carro	Homicidio	Rápido
Circunstancial	Hospital	Respiración
Conducta	Identificación	Silencio
Contradictorio	Importante	Teléfono
Corte *- Court*	Inglés	Terrible
Droga	Insignia	Víctima

Muchos Ways to "Practicar"

The more you listen to and use your *español,* the easier it will be for you to learn. There are lots of creative ways to practice that won't cost you any money. Try these super techniques for improving your skills:

✓ Next time you're at a Mexican restaurant, order your food in *español.*

✓ Start slowly. Practice one sound each week.

✓ Read Spanish language newspapers. They are usually free and easily available.

✓ Listen to Spanish language radio stations.

✓ Watch Spanish language television.

✓ Rent Spanish language videos — especially cartoons.

✓ Buy Spanish tapes and listen to them in the car while you commute.

✓ Speaking of tapes, there is such a variety of Latin *música* available, something will be right for you. Listening to music is a great way to train your ears to Spanish and have fun doing it. Personally, I like anything by Carlos Santana or Marc Anthony. What do you like?

✓ Visit Internet sites such as *www.about.com* or *www.studyspanish.com.* You will find all kinds of information about the Spanish language. They have a wonderful, free newsletter that is sent via e-mail. Most search engines also have a Spanish section of some sort. An on-line search will turn up lots of treasures!

✓ Next time you listen to a baseball game, keep track of all the Hispanic names you hear.

✓ Speak Spanish every time the opportunity presents itself. Practice is the only way to overcome your nervousness.

✓ Learn with a friend at work and practice together.

SpeakEasy's Tips and Techniques for Comunicación

When you're trying to communicate with a person who is "limited in English proficiency", it's important to remember that *patience is a virtue*! Put yourself in their shoes, and contemplate how you would feel if the roles were reversed. Here are some easy things you can do to make the conversation easier for both of you.

- ✓ Speak slowly and distinctly.
- ✓ Do not use slang expressions or colorful terms.
- ✓ Get straight to the point! Unnecessary words cloud your meaning.
- ✓ Speak in a normal tone. Speaking *loudly* doesn't help anyone understand you any better!
- ✓ Look for visual cues in body language and facial expressions. Use gestures of your own to get your point across.
- ✓ You may not receive good eye contact. Do not interpret the lack of eye contact negatively.
- ✓ Given that Latinos tend to stand closer to each other than North Americans when they talk to each other, your personal space could feel crowded. Stand your ground!
- ✓ Feel free to use gestures and body language of your own to communicate.
- ✓ Because of the way languages are learned, it is likely that the person you are talking to understands more of what you are saying than he is able to verbalize. *So, be careful what you say!* No matter what the language, we always understand the bad words first!

Tips & Tidbits

Throughout your book, look for the light bulb you see above. This section will provide helpful hints and cultural information designed to help you learn Spanish more easily.

Beginning Words & Phrases

Let's get started! In no time at all, you will begin to gain confidence. Your Latino colleagues and clients will be delighted you are learning to speak *español*. Even if you can't remember a whole phrase, *por favor* use the words you know. Words like "please" and "thank you" show politeness and respect. Courtesy goes a long way towards establishing a good rapport.

English	Español	Guide
Hi!	¡Hola!	OH-la
How are you?	¿Cómo está?	KO-mo es-TA
Fine	Muy bien.	mooy b-N
So so	Así así	ah-SEE ah-SEE
Bad	Mal	mal
Good morning	Buenos días	boo-WAY-nos DEE-ahs
Good afternoon	Buenas tardes	boo-WAY-nas TAR-days
Good night	Buenas noches.	boo-WAY-nas NO-chase
Sir or Mister	Señor	sen-YOUR
Mrs. or Ma'am	Señora	sen-YOUR-ah
Miss	Señorita	sen-your-REE-ta
What's your name?	¿Cómo se llama?	KO-mo say YA-ma
My name is ___.	Me llamo ____.	may YA-mo
Nice to meet you.	¡Mucho gusto!	MOO-cho GOO-stow
Thank you.	Gracias.	GRA-see-ahs
Please!	¡Por favor!	pour-fa-VOR
You're welcome.	De nada.	day NA da
I'm sorry.	Lo siento.	low-see-N-toe
Excuse me.	¡Perdón!	pear-DON
Good-bye	Adiós	ah-dee-OS

Spanish Sounds Rápido — What Do I Do Now?

Be honest! One of the reasons you are hesitant to speak Spanish is that the language sounds so fast! Naturally, you're afraid you won't understand. Here are some phrases that will help you; make learning them a priority. *¿Comprende, amigo?*

[handwritten: Pochito - Smidge - Very Small Amt]

[handwritten in left margin: A - you O - I]

[handwritten in left margin: AEIO Short Vowels]

English	Español	Guide
I don't understand.	No comprendo.	no com-**PREN**-doe
Do you understand?	¿Comprende?	com-**PREN**-day
I speak a little Spanish.	Hablo poco español.	**AH**-blow **POE**-co es-pan-**NYOL**
Do you speak English?	¿Habla inglés?	**AH**-bla eng-**LACE**
Repeat please.	Repita por favor.	ray-**PETE**-ah pour fa-**VOR**
Write it please.	Escribe por favor.	es-**SCRE**-bay pour fa-**VOR**
Speak more slowly please.	Habla más despacio por favor.	**AH**-bla mas des-**PA**-see-oh pour fa-**VOR**
Thanks for your patience.	Gracias por su paciencia.	**GRA**-see-ahs pour sue pa-see-**N**-see-ah
How do you say it in Spanish?	¿Como se dice en español?	**CO**-mo say **DEE**-say n es-pan-**NYOL**
Where are you from?	¿De dónde es?	day **DON**-day es
May I help you?	¿Puedo servirle?	pooh-**A**-doe seer-**VEER**-lay

The key here is <u>not</u> to pánico.

The person you are speaking Spanish with is having just as much trouble understanding you, as you are having understanding them! Hang in there! Between the two of you, *comunicación* will begin to take place.

15

SpeakEasy's Conversaciones

Practice Conversation I

USTED (YOU):   Good morning, Sir.

SR. GARCÍA   Good morning. How are you?

USTED   Fine, thanks. How are you?

SR. GARCÍA   OK, thanks.

Practice Conversation II

USTED: May I help you? My name is

_____. I speak a little Spanish.

What's your name?

SRA. GARCÍA: My name is Carla García-

Hernandez. I speak a little English.

USTED: Nice to meet you.

SRA. GARCÍA: Yes, nice to meet you.

Using phrases found on pages 14-15, can you say the following?

✓ A greeting of your choice.

✓ My name is _____.

✓ I speak a little Spanish.

✓ Do you speak English?

✓ Speak more slowly, please.

✓ Thank you

¿Cuál Es Su Nombre Completo?

What Is Your <u>Complete</u> Name?

Hispanic Names Have Four Parts

First Name	Middle Name	Father's Surname	Mother's Surname
Primer Nombre	Segundo Nombre	Apellido Paterno	Apellido Materno
Carlos	Jesús	Santana	Rodríguez
Poncho	Luis	Villa	García
Carmen	Elena	Miranda	Rivera

Start with: Señor, Señora,   or   Señorita

Use Both Names Or Only The Father's Last Name

Sr. Santana   Sr. Villa   Sra. Miranda

When A Woman Marries

She <u>keeps</u> her father's **Apellido Paterno**, and she <u>drops</u> her **Apellido Materno**
In place of her **Apellido Materno** is her husband's **Apellido Paterno**

Children Have The Apellido Paterno of
Both Father and Mother

*If Carlos Santana married Carmen Miranda Rivera,
what would her name be after the marriage? What's the complete name
of their child?*

José Carlos ???? ?????

Answer: Carmen Miranda-Santana José Carlos Santana Miranda

Spanish Nouns
Can words *really* have a gender?

¡*Sí*! Spanish belongs to the "romance" language family. It doesn't have anything to do with love, but it has a lot to do with the Romans. In ancient times, people had the same trouble learning languages that they do today, except there were no cassette tapes, CDs, PDAs or many foreign language teachers. In those days, there weren't even many schools for that matter! Consequently, most folks were on their own when it came to learning another language.

To help the difficult process along, words were placed into categories based upon how they sounded. This process organized the material and made it easier to learn. Old world languages had categories that were often described as "masculine," "feminine," or even "neutral." From these descriptions, people began talking about words in terms of their gender. Even though the word "gender" is misleading, the tendency to group words by sound helped people learn new languages more quickly.

NOUN

A person, place or thing

Because Spanish evolved from Latin, it has maintained two category divisions for thousands of years. The categories are called masculine and feminine. Even though Spanish can and will evolve, the concept of categories in *español* is unlikely to change.

Here are the most important points to remember about nouns and their categories:

1. Usually, the words are grouped by how they sound, not by what they mean. There will always be a few exceptions!

2. Languages are a lot like the people who use them: They don't always follow the rules!

3. If the Spanish noun is referring to a person, the letter will often indicate the sex of that individual. For example: a doctor, who is a man, is a "*doctor*," while a woman, who is a doctor, is a "*doctora*."

4. Words in the "masculine" category usually end with the letter "O".

5. Words in the "feminine" category usually end with the letter "A".

6. El, la, los and las are very important words. They all mean "the". They are the clues you need to tell you a word's category.

El (masculine category – singular)   El niño, El muchacho
Los (masculine category – plural)   Los niños, Los muchachos
La (feminine category – singular)   La niña, La muchacha
Las (feminine category – plural)   Las niñas, Las muchachas

A Word about Adjectives

Describing things in Spanish can present problems for English speakers. There are several reasons why using adjectives may give us trouble. First, there is the position of the adjective in relation to the noun. In English, descriptive words go in front of the noun like "white cat," for example. In Spanish, the noun is the most important element, so it comes first. White cat is *gato blanco* — the word order is opposite to English. However, it gets more complicated because there are a few basic adjectives which show size or quantity that are placed in front of the noun, just as in English. These include words such as large (*grande*) and small (*pequeño*), along with numbers. For example: a large white cat is *un grande gato blanco*.

Second, since Spanish nouns are divided into masculine and feminine categories, the adjective must match its noun by category. This means that from time to time you will need to match the letter at the end of the adjective and make it the same letter as the one at the end of the noun. You must also match the adjective to the noun by number (singular or plural). This matching sound feature of Spanish is one of the main reasons the language has such a musical quality.

19

Here are several examples:

One large white cat = *Uno grande gato blanco*
Three large white cats = *Tres grandes gatos blancos.*

One large white house = *Una grande casa blanca*
Six large white houses = *Seis grandes casas blancas*

Common Adjectives — Adjectivos Comunes

These common adjectives are shown as you would find them in a Spanish dictionary. As written, use them with singular words in the masculine category, and place them behind the noun. Change the "o" at the end to an "a" to make them match up with words in the feminine category. Don't forget to add an "s" at the end for plural words.

English	Español	English	Español
Good	Bueno	Bad	Malo
Better	Mejor	Worse	Peor
Big	Grande	Small	Pequeño
Clean	Limpio	Dirty	Sucio
Hot	Caliente	Cold	Frío
Safe	Seguro	Dangerous	Peligroso
Easy	Fácil	Difficult	Difícil
Full	Lleno	Empty	Vacío
Fast	Rápido	Slow	Lento
Hard	Duro	Soft	Blando
New	Nuevo	Old	Viejo
Pretty	Bonito	Ugly	Feo
Quiet	Tranquilo	Restless	Inquieto
Tall	Alto	Short	Bajo
Well	Bien	Sick	Enfermo
Strong	Fuerte	Weak	Débil

The Essentials of Spanish Verbs

There are basically three types of regular verbs in Spanish. The last two letters on the end of the verb determines how the word is to be treated. Listed below are the three most common types of regular verb endings.

- ✓ AR – Hablar: To speak
- ✓ ER – Comprender: To understand
- ✓ IR – Escribir: To write

In survival Spanish, we focus on speaking about ourselves and talking to another person. That's the most common type of "one-on-one" communication.

When you need to say "I speak," "I understand," or "I live," change the last two letters of the verb to an "O".

- ✓ Hablo
- ✓ Comprendo
- ✓ Escribo

When asking a question such as "do you speak," "do you understand," or "do you live," change the ending to an "a" or an "e". *The change in letter indicates that you are speaking to someone else.*

- ✓ Habla
- ✓ Comprende
- ✓ Escribe

To make a sentence negative, simply put "no" in front of the verb.

- ✓ No hablo.
- ✓ No comprendo.
- ✓ No escribo.

VERB: Shows action or state of being

¡Acción!

There are so many English friendly *acción* words in the Spanish "AR" verb family. Many of them bear a strong resemblance to English verbs — most of them share a simple, regular nature. They are a very important asset in on-the-job communication. We picked a few of our favorites to get you started. Look closely at the list on the next page. On it, you will recognize many comforting similarities between our languages that are also practical! Changing one letter will really expand your conversational skills.

In on-the-job conversations, people tend to use "I" and "you" to start many sentences. Of all the pronouns, these two are the most powerful and will work best for you, so that's where we will start.

Here's an important difference between our languages — in English, the use of pronouns is essential because most of our verbs tend to end the same way. For example, with "I speak" and "you speak" the verb "speak" remains the same. In English, our pronouns make all the difference. Spanish is different in this aspect. Spanish-speaking people are listening for the letters at the end of the verb. That's what indicates who or what is being talked about in Spanish. Each ending is different. The ending of the Spanish verb is much more important than the beginning. The ending of the verb tells the Spanish-speaking person who, or what, is being discussed. In most cases when people speak Spanish, you might not hear a pronoun. It's not necessary for precise meaning. That's a big reason why Spanish might sound a little fast to you: *Pronouns which are important in English are routinely eliminated in Spanish!*

Try this: Treat the verbs in the "AR" family as you would "to speak" or "hablar." End the verb with an "o" when you're talking about yourself; "hablo" or "I speak". Change the verb ending from an "o" to an "a" for "habla" or "you speak." Use this form when you're talking to someone else.

English	Español	Guide
I need	Necesito	nay-say-**SEE**-toe
You need	Necesita	nay-say-**SEE**-ta

The Sweet 16 Verbs

English	Español	Guide
1. To need	Necesitar	nay-say-see-**TAR**
2. To use	Usar	oo-**SAR**
3. To prepare	Preparar	pray-pa-**RAR**
4. To accept	Aceptar	ah-sep-**TAR**
5. To work	Trabajar	tra-baa-**HAR**
6. To analyze	Analizar	ah-nal-lee-**SAR**
7. To call	Llamar	ya-**MAR**
8. To observe	Observar	ob-ser-**VAR**
9. To insult	Insultar	een-sool-**TAR**
10. To ask	Preguntar	prey-goon-**TAR**
11. To carry	Llevar	yea-**VAR**
12. To evacuate	Evacuar	a-vah-coo-**ARE**
13. To cooperate	Cooperar	co-op-air-**RAR**
14. To inform	Informar	een-for-**MAR**
15. To pay	Pagar	pa-**GAR**
16. To return	Regresar	ray-grey-**SAR**

**Note: To make a sentence negative, say no in front of the verb.
   Example: I don't need. **No necesito.** You don't need **No necesita.**

Tips and Tidbits

In conversation, most Spanish-speaking people omit the use of pronouns such as "I" and "you." In English, pronouns are very important because many of our verb forms sound the same. All the verbs in Spanish sound *muy diferente*.

Which verbs in the Sweet 16 do you use most often? List your top four:

1. _____

2. _____

3. _____

4. _____

Now take your top five and change the AR ending to an "a" to indicate you are talking to someone else. Example: habla, meaning you speak.

1. _____

2. _____

3. _____

4. _____

5. _____

¡Necesito una breaka! ¿Y usted?

Ready for More Acción?

Verbs or action words are the essential tools of language. Every sentence needs at least one. Here is a dictionary of common verbs you will need on your job. The best way to begin learning these verbs is to go through the list first and find all the English to Spanish matches. Those will be the easiest to remember because of their striking similarity to *inglés*. Be aware, however, that you will also meet some false friends along the way. These are words like "*molestar*," which means "to bother" instead of "to molest."

After you have looked for strong relationships between English and Spanish verbs, the next step is to look at the ending of each verb. This will determine how you treat the word in conversation. Go back to "The Essentials of Spanish Grammar" on page 21 for more *información* on how to manipulate the endings to make them work for you.

The last step in preparing yourself to learn these important words is to go through the list again highlighting the words you will use most often. Start with ten and practice them regularly. When you feel that you can use the words, take on 10 more. Work your way through the list a little bit at a time until you have learned them all.

Here's another great tip for using action words in conversation. Any time you would start a sentence with please, you can use the Spanish phrase "favor de." Follow that up with any of the verbs from the list just as they are. Using that phrase, you can include the verbs without having to change them at all. Here are some examples:

Please speak English.
Favor de hablar inglés.

Please write your full name.
Favor de escribir su nombre completo.

English	Español	Guide
TO.....		
Abuse	Abusar	ah-boo-**SAR**
Accuse	Acusar	ah-coo-**SAR**
Answer	Contestar	con-test-**TAR**
Arrest	Arrestar	ah-rest-**TAR**
Arrive	Llegar	yea-**GAR**
Ask	Preguntar	pray-goon-**TAR**
Attend	Asistir	ah-cease-**TIER**
Begin	Comenzar	co-men-**SAR**
Bend	Doblar	doe-**BLAR**
Bleed	Sangrar	san-**GRAR**
Blow	Soplar	so-**PLAR**
Bother	Molestar	mo-les-**TAR**
Break in	Forzar	for-**SAR**
Breathe	Respirar	rays-pee-**RAR**
Call	Llamar	ya-**MAR**
Calm	Calmar	cal-**MAR**
Carry	Llevar	yea-**VAR**
Charge	Denunciar	day-newn-see-**ARE**
Check	Verificar	ver-ree-fee-**CAR**
Clean	Limpiar	leem-pee-**ARE**
Consume	Tomar	toe-**MAR**
Continue	Continuar	con-teen-oo-**ARE**
Crash	Chocar	cho-**CAR**
Cry	Llorar	yo-**RARE**

English	Español	Guide
Cut	Cortar	core-**TAT**
Detain	Detener	day-ten-**NAIR**
Die	Morir	more-**REAR**
Drink	Beber	bay-**BEAR**
Drive	Manejar	man-nay-**HAR**
End	Terminar	ter-me-**NAR**
Escape	Escapar	ace-ca-**PARE**
Examine	Examinar	ax-ah-me-**NAR**
Fight	Pelear	pay-lay-**ARE**
Find	Encontrar	n-cont-**RARE**
Frighten	Asustar	ah-seus-**TAR**
Frisk	Registrar	ray-hees-**TRAR**
Happen	Pasar	pa-**SAR**
Help	Ayudar	eye-oo-**DAR**
Hide	Esconder	ace-con-**DARE**
Hit	Pegar	pay-**GAR**
Impound	Embargar	m-bar-**GAR**
Incarcerate	Encarcelar	n-car-cell-**ARE**
Inhale	Inhalar	n-ah-**LAR**
Inject	Inyectar	n-yec-**TAR**
Injure	Herir	air-**REAR**
Investigate	Investigar	n-ves-tee-**GAR**
Kill	Matar	ma-**TAR**
Lift	Levantar	lay-van-**TAR**
Listen	Escuchar	ace-coo-**CHAR**

English	Español	Guide
Look at	Mirar	me-**RARE**
Murder	Matar	ma-**TAR**
Obey	Obedecer	oh-bay-day-**SER**
Obstruct	Obstruir	ob-strew-**EAR**
Park	Estacionar	ace-sta-see-on-**NAR**
Protect	Proteger	pro-tay-**HAIR**
Pull	Jalar	ha-**LAR**
Punish	Castigar	ca-stee-**GAR**
Push	Empujar	m-poo-**HAR**
Rape	Violar	vee-oh-**LAR**
Recover	Recuperar	ray-coo-pear-**RAR**
Refuse	Rehusar	ray-oo-**SAR**
Repeat	Repetir	ray-pay-**TEER**
Report	Reportar	ray-por-**TAR**
Reserve	Reservar	ray-ser-**VAR**
Respond	Responder	ray-spon-**DARE**
Rest	Descansar	days-can-**SAR**
Search	Buscar	boos-**CAR**
Serve	Servir	ser-**VEER**
Sex	Tener relaciones sexuales	ten-**AIR** ray-la-see-**ON**-ace sex-oo-**AL**-ace
Shoot	Disparar	dees-pa-**RARE**
Sign	Firmar	fear-**MAR**
Signal	Señalar	sen-yal-**ARE**
Sit down	Sentarse	sen-**TAR**-say

English	Español	Guide
Stand up	Levantarse	lay-van-**TAR**-say
Steal	Robar	ro-**BAR**
Stop	Parar	pa-**RARE**
Suffer	Sufrir	souf-**REAR**
Surround	Rodear	ro-day-**AIR**
Suspend	Suspender	seus-pen-**DARE**
Swallow	Tragar	tra-**GAR**
Swerve	Zigzaguear	seeg-sa-gay-**ARE**
Take place	Suceder	sue-say-**DARE**
Take	Tomar	to-**MAR**
Talk	Hablar	ah-**BLAR**
Threaten	Amenazar	ah-may-na-**SAR**
Touch	Tocar	to-**CAR**
Tow	Remolcar	ray-mol-**CAR**
Turn oneself	Darse vuelta	**DAR**-say voo-ale-**TA**
Understand	Comprender	com-pren-**DARE**
	Entender	n-ten-**DARE**
Use	Usar	oo-**SAR**
Vomit	Vomitar	vo-me-**TAR**
Walk	Caminar	ca-me-**NAR**
Warn	Advertir	ad-ver-**TEER**
Work	Trabajar	tra-ba-**HAR**
Wreck	Arruinar	ah-rue-een-**NAR**
Write	Escribir	ace-cree-**BEER**
Yell	Gritar	gree-**TAR**

Irregular Verbs: The Big Five

Now that you have had the opportunity to learn about the tremendous number of verbs that follow regular patterns in Spanish, it's time to take a look at others that don't follow the rules. They are unpredictable, but they are very important. In fact, they reflect some of man's oldest concepts. That's why they tend to be irregular. These words were in use long before language rules and patterns were set. There are two verbs in Spanish that mean "to be." The others are: "to have," "to make" and "to go." Because they don't follow the rules, you will need to memorize them. However, that should be easy because you will use and hear them often.

In English, the "to be" verb is "I am," "you are," "he is" etc. The Spanish version is **ser** and **estar**. *Ser* is used to express permanent things such as your nationality or profession. *Estar* is used when talking about location or conditions that change such as a person's health.

Ser		Estar	
Yo **soy**	Nosotros **somos**	Yo **estoy**	Nosotros **estamos**
Tú **eres**		Tú **estás**	
Él **es**	Ellos **son**	Él **está**	Ellos **están**
Ella **es**	Ellas **son**	Ella **está**	Ellas **están**
Usted **es**	Ustedes **son**	Usted **está**	Ustedes **están**

The verb *"to have"* in Spanish, is *muy importante*. In English, we say that we are hot, cold, hungry, thirsty, right, wrong or sleepy, but in Spanish, these are conditions that you have. Some of the expressions mean something totally different than expected if you confuse the verbs, so be careful!

Tener	
Yo **tengo**	Nosotros **tenemos**
Tú **tienes**	
Él **tiene**	Ellos **tienen**
Ella **tiene**	Ellas **tienen**
Usted **tiene**	Ustedes **tienen**

In Spanish, the verb that means *"to do"* also means *"to make."* It's not unusual for one verb to have multiple meanings. There are many expressions that require the use of this verb, but you will use it most when you talk about the weather. That's a safe subject and one that everyone worldwide discusses! **¿Qué tiempo hace?** What's the weather? **Hace frío.** (It's cold.) **Hace sol.** (It's sunny). **Hace calor.** (It's hot) **Hace viento** (It's windy.). Here are two exceptions: **Está lloviendo.** (It's raining.) and **Está nevando.** (It's snowing.)

Hacer

Yo **hago**	Nosotros **hacemos**
Tú **haces**	
Él **hace**	Ellos **hacen**
Ella **hace**	Ellas **hacen**
Usted **hace**	Ustedes **hacen.**

The last of the big five is perhaps the easiest to use. It's the verb that means, *"to go"*. In Spanish, the verb is *ir* which is pronounced like the English word "ear." In both English and Spanish, we use parts of the word to make the future tense or to talk about things that we are going to do. Look at the parts of *ir*. Now look back at the parts of the verb *ser*. Do you notice any similarities?

Ir

Yo **voy**	Nosotros **vamos**
Tú **vas**	
Él **va**	Ellos **van**
Ella **va**	Ellas **van**
Usted **va**	Ustedes **van**

When you want to say something that you are going to do, start with "I'm going" or *voy*. Next, insert the word "*a*," and the basic verb that states what it is that you're going to do. Try it! It's easy. Here are some examples.

Voy a visitar a mi familia.	I am going to visit my family.
Voy a organizar el grupo.	I am going to organize the group.
Mario va a comprar la medicina.	Mario is going to buy the medicine.

Note: The whole concept of irregular verbs can be quite daunting. Don't let it defeat you! We have many irregular verbs in English. Every language has them. The only way to master them is to use them. Make them your own! Try writing different parts of a verb on your desk calendar. That way, the words will be right in front of you every time you look down. When you see a word, say it to yourself. You will have it conquered in no time.

Are you hungry? — ¿Tiene hambre?

Using the right verb at the right time is very important. The following common expressions in Spanish require the use of *tener*. These are phrases you must learn, even though the translation will feel strange to you. *Remember our English idioms often sound very strange to others.*

As a rule, *tener* is used to describe physical conditions. In English, we use the verb *to be.*

TENER: To have   **TENGO: I have**   **TIENE: You have**

English	Español	Guide
Hot	Calor	ca-**LORE**
Hungry	Hambre	**AM**-bray
Cold	Frío.	**FREE**-oh
Ashamed	Vergüenza	ver-goo-**N**-sa
In pain.	Dolor	doe-**LORE**
Afraid of	Miedo de	me-**A**-doe day
Right	Razón	rah-**SEWN**
Thirsty	Sed	said
Sleepy	Sueño	soo-**WAYNE**-nyo
xx years old	*xx* años	xx **AHN**-nyos

What's the Weather? — ¿Qué tiempo hace?

A general topic for discussion in any culture is always the weather. Discussing the weather in Spanish requires a different verb from the one used in English. If you say to your host, "*Está frío*," he or she would think that you were talking about something you had touched. In Spanish, use the verb **hacer** which means "to do" or "to make" to describe the weather. This verb is one of the big five irregulars.

English	Español	Guide
To be nice weather	Hace buen tiempo	AH-say boo-WAYNE
To be hot	Hace calor	AH-say ca-LORE
To be cool	Hace fresco	AH-say FRES-co
To be sunny	Hace sol	AH-say sol
To be windy	Hace viento	AH-say v-N-toe
To be cold	Hace frío	AH-say FREE-oh
Rain	Lluvia	U-v-ah
To rain	Llover	YO-ver
What's the weather?	¿Qué tiempo hace?	kay t-M-poe AH-say

Tips & Tidbits

In North America, we use the Fahrenheit scale for measuring the temperature. Latin American countries use the Celsius scale. What's the difference? Here's a simple example: 0 degrees Celsius is 32 degrees Fahrenheit.

Special Uses of Ser and Estar

The verbs *ser* and *estar* both mean the same thing in English: *to be,* but *how can two verbs mean the same thing?* It's because *ser* and *estar* are used in very different ways. Spanish sees these two verbs differently and uses them in very precise ways. Listed below are some simple guidelines on their usage:

COMMON USES OF SER

A.   To express an permanent quality or characteristic

     La puerta es de madera.   The door is made of wood.

     El hospital es enorme.   The hospital is enormous.

     Los doctores son importantes.   Doctors are important.

B.   To describe or identify

     Mi amigo es médico.   My friend is a doctor.

     El estudiante es alto.   The student is tall.

C.   To indicate nationality

     Pedro es mexicano.   Pedro is Mexican.

     La historia es de Argentina.   The story is from Argentina.

D.   To express ownership

     Este es mi auto.   This is my car.

     Este es mi libro.   This is my book.

E.   To express time and dates

     ¿Qué hora es?   What time is it?

     Hoy es el nueve de junio.   Today is the 9th of June.

F.	With impersonal expressions.

Es importante estudiar.　　　It's important to study.

Es necesario leer.　　　It's necessary to read.

COMMON USES OF ESTAR

A.	To express location

Estoy en la oficina.　　　I am in the office.

Charlotte está en Carolina del Norte.　Charlotte is in North Carolina.

El baño está en el segundo piso.　The bathroom is on the 2nd floor.

B.	To indicate someone's health

Mi esposa está enferma.　　　My wife is sick.

¿Cómo está usted?　　　How are you?

C.	*Estar* is also used as a helping verb

Estoy hablando.　　　I am speaking.

Carmen está trabajando.　　　Carmen is working.

Julio está regresando mañana.　Julio is returning tomorrow.

Tips & Tidbits

Notice from the examples that *ser* is used more frequently than *estar*. Even though the usage of *ser* and *estar* seems complicated in the beginning, both verbs are used so frequently in conversation that you will quickly become comfortable using them. In most cases, you will be understood, even if you use the wrong one.

The Numbers — Los Números

Number	Español	Guide
0	Cero	SAY-row
1	Uno	OO-no
2	Dos	dose
3	Tres	trays
4	Cuatro	coo-AH-trow
5	Cinco	SINK-oh
6	Seis	SAY-ees
7	Siete	see-A-tay
8	Ocho	OH-cho
9	Nueve	new-A-vay
10	Diez	d-ACE
11	Once	ON-say
12	Doce	DOSE-a
13	Trece	TRAY-say
14	Catorce	ca-TOR-say
15	Quince	KEEN-say
16	Diez y seis	d-ACE e SAY-ees
17	Diez y siete	d-ACE e see-ATE-tay
18	Diez y ocho	d-ACE e OH-cho
19	Diez y nueve	d-ACE e new-A-vay
20	Veinte	VAIN-tay
21	Veinte y uno	VAIN-tay e OO-no
22	Veinte y dos	VAIN-tay e dose
23	Veinte y tres	VAIN-tay e trays
24	Veinte y cuatro	VAIN-tay e coo-AH-trow
25	Veinte y cinco	VAIN-tay e SINK-oh
26	Veinte y seis	VAIN-tay e SAY-ees
27	Veinte y siete	VAIN-tay e see-A-tay
28	Veinte y ocho	VAIN-tay e OH-cho -
29	Veinte y nueve	VAIN-tay e new-A-vay
30	Treinta	TRAIN-ta
40	Cuarenta	kwah-RAIN-ta

Number	Español	Guide
50	Cincuenta	seen-**KWAIN**-ta
60	Sesenta	say-**SAIN**-ta
70	Setenta	say-**TAIN**-ta
80	Ochenta	oh-**CHAIN**-ta
90	Noventa	no-**VAIN**-ta
100	Cien	see-**IN**
200	Doscientos	dose-see-**N**-toes
300	Trescientos	tray-see-**N**-toes
400	Cuatrocientos	coo-**AH**-troh-see-**N**-toes
500	Quinientos	keen-e-**N**-toes
600	Seiscientos	**SAY**-ees-see-**N**-toes
700	Setecientos	**SAY**-tay-see-**N**-toes
800	Ochocientos	**OH**-choh- see-**N**-toes
900	Novecientos	**NO**-vay-see-**N**-toes
1,000	Mil	meal

Tips and Tidbits

When you are talking with a native speaker and you are discussing anything involving numbers, keep the following important information in mind:

1. Most people say numbers *extremely* fast! Don't hesitate to ask for a number to be said more slowly or to be repeated. Review the chapter called *Spanish Sounds Rápido — What Do I Do Now?*

2. When native speakers say their phone numbers, they will often pair the numbers together instead of saying them as single digits.

3. If you are expressing a date which contains the year, a native speaker will often say the complete number. For example: 1962 will be said "one thousand nine hundred sixty and two" or "*mil novecientos sesenta y dos.*" If you wish, it is also correct to pair the numbers as "nineteen sixty-two" or "*diez y nueve sesenta y dos.*"

Days of the Week and Months of the Year
Los Días de la Semana

English	Español	Guide
Monday	lunes	**LOON**-ace
Tuesday	martes	**MAR**-tays
Wednesday	miércoles	me-**AIR**-co-lace
Thursday	jueves	who-**WAVE**-ace
Friday	viernes	v-**AIR**-nace
Saturday	sábado	**SAH**-ba-doe
Sunday	domingo	doe-**MING**-go

When expressing a date in Spanish, give the number of the day first.
Follow the day with the month. Use the following format:
El (date) de (month).

Los Meses del Año

English	Español	Guide
January	enero	n-**NAY**-row
February	febrero	fay-**BRAY**-row
March	marzo	**MAR**-so
April	abril	ah-**BRILL**
May	mayo	**MY**-oh
June	junio	**WHO**-knee-oh
July	julio	**WHO**-lee-oh
August	agosto	ah-**GOSE**-toe
September	septiembre	sep-tee-**EM**-bray
October	octubre	oc-**TOO**-bray
November	noviembre	no-v-**EM**-bray
December	diciembre	d-see-**EM**-bray

Your appointment is (*day of the week*) el (*number*) de (*month*).
Su cita es lunes, el 11 de octubre.

What Time Is It? — ¿Qué Hora Es?

The concept of time is something that varies from culture to culture. Many countries place less emphasis on being on time for certain things than Americans. In Latino culture, most people live for the present. It can be especially true in one's personal life; however, on the job, everyone knows the value of *puntualidad*. *¡Es muy importante!*

Learning to tell time is another good way to put your Spanish numbers to good use *¿Qué hora es?* means *what time is it?*

It's one o'clock.	Es la una.
It's two o'clock.	Son las dos.
It's 3:30.	Son las tres y media.
It's 5:45.	Son las seis menos quince.

Use the phrases *de la mañana* to indicate morning, and *de la tarde* to indicate afternoon. In addition, midnight is *medianoche* and noon is *mediodía*.

To find out at what time something takes place, ask: *¿A qué hora...?*

¿A qué hora es la reunión?	What time is the meeting?
¿A qué hora termina?	What time do you finish?

Spanish speakers sometimes use the 24-hour clock for departures and arrivals such as trains and flights.

12:05	las doce cero cinco
17.52	las diez y siete cincuenta y dos

Para Practicar

Using the word for meeting *"la reunion,"* say your meeting takes place on the hour throughout your workday. *La reunión es a las ocho.*

39

Scheduling an Appointment

When you need to schedule an appointment, this form will come in very handy. In *español,* an appointment is called a *cita* (**SEE**-ta). First, list the name of the individual with whom the appointment is made. Then circle the day of the week, followed by the number for the day. Finally, circle the month and add the time. The phrase at the bottom of this form simply asks the individual to arrive ten minutes early for the appointment.

Usted tiene una cita importante con _____.

La cita es   lunes   el _____ de   enero   a las _____.

             martes   febrero

             miércoles   marzo

             jueves   abril

             viernes   mayo

                                               junio

                                               julio

                                               agosto

                                               septiembre

                                               octubre

                                               noviembre

                                               diciembre

***Favor de llegar 10 minutos antes del tiempo de su cita. ¡Gracias!*

Please arrive 10 minutes before the time of your appointment. Thank you.

The Questions Everyone Should Know

English	Español	Guide
Who?	¿Quién?	key-N
What?	¿Qué?	kay
Which?	¿Cuál?	coo-**ALL**
When?	¿Cuándo?	**KWAN**-doe
Where?	¿Dónde?	**DON**-day
Why?	¿Por qué?	pour **KAY**
How?	¿Cómo?	**CO**-mo
What's happening?	¿Qué pasa?	kay **PA**-sa
How much?	¿Cuánto?	**KWAN**-toe
How many?	¿Cuántos?	**KWAN**-toes

When you ask a question in Spanish, it will take on the same form as a question in English. Start with the question word that asks the information you need. Follow the question word with a verb, and give your voice an upward inflection.

In Spanish, you can also make a question by ending your sentence with ¿no? Here's an example: *Cancún está en México, ¿no?* When you end a sentence with "no" like this, it takes on the meaning of "isn't it."

The Most Common Questions

How are you?   ¿Cómo está?
How much does it cost?   ¿Cuánto cuesta?
Where are you from?   ¿De dónde es?

To make the Spanish upside down question mark or the upside down exclamation mark refer, to the chapter called "Typing in Spanish on Your Computer."

Getting the Información

Listed below are common phrases that are used to fill out almost any questionnaire. It seems like most forms ask for much of the same information in almost the same order. By learning a few simple phrases, you can use this format to your advantage.

There are so many times when we need to ask for very basic information. Most of these questions begin with the words *"what is your."* When you are asking this type of question, remember that it's not always necessary to form a complete sentence to have good communication. The information you are asking for is much more important than the phrase "what is your"? As long as you remember to make what you say *sound* like a question by giving your voice an *upward* inflection, people will interpret what you've said *as* a question.

Use the form on the following page; it asks for very basic information. To help you practice, work with a partner. Make up new information about yourself and complete the form. At each practice session, one of you will ask the questions and the other will provide the answers to fill in the information requested. This is a great practice exercise — most of the time the questions you ask will be the same, but the answers you receive will always be different!

What's your. . .

¿Cuál es su. . .
coo-ALL es sue

English	Español	Guide
Full name	Nombre completo	NOM-bray com-**PLAY**-toe
First name	Primer nombre	pre-**MARE** NOM-bray
Middle name	Segundo nombre	say-**GOON**-doe NOM-bray
Last name (surname)	Apellido	ah-pay-**YE**-doe

English	Español	Guide
Paternal surname	Apellido paterno	ah-pay-**YE**-doe pa-**TER**-no
Maternal surname	Apellido materno	ah-pay-**YE**-doe ma-**TER**-no
Address	Dirección	d-wreck-see-**ON**
Apartment number	Número de apartamento	**NEW**-may-row day ah-par-ta-**MEN**-toe
Age	Edad	a-**DAD**
Date of birth	Fecha de nacimiento	**FAY**-cha day na-see-me-**N**-toe
Nationality	Nacionalidad	na-see-on-nal-e-**DAD**
Place of birth	Lugar de nacimiento	loo-**GAR** day na-see-me-**N**-toe
Place of employment	Lugar de empleo	loo-**GAR** day m-**PLAY**-oh
Occupation	Ocupación	oh-coo-pa-see-**ON**
Home telephone number	Número de teléfono de su casa	**NEW**-may-row day tay-**LAY**-fo-no day sue **CA**-sa
Work telephone number	Número de teléfono de su empleo	**NEW**-may-row day tay-**LAY**-fo-no day sue m-**PLAY**-oh
Marital status	Estado civil	es-**TA**-doe see-**VEAL**
Married	Casado *(a)*	ca-**SA**-doe
Single	Soltero *(a)*	soul-**TAY**-row
Divorced	Divorciado *(a)*	d-vor-see-**AH**-doe
Widow	Viudo *(a)*	v-**OO**-doe
Separated	Separado *(a)*	sep-pa-**RAH**-doe
Driver's license number	Número de licencia	**NEW**-may-row day lee-**SEN**-see-ah
Social security number	Número de seguro social	**NEW**-may-row day say-**GOO**-row sew-see-**AL**

Información Básica
Imprima por favor

Fecha: _____
          Mes   Día   Año

Sr.
Sra.
Srta._____
_____Primer Nombre_____Segundo Nombre_____Apellido Paterno_____Apellido Materno (Esposo)

Dirección:_____
_____Calle

_____
Ciudad_____Estado_____Zona postal

Teléfono: Casa _____   Empleo_____

          Cel_____   Fax _____

Correo electrónico _____

Número de seguro social: _____-_____-_____

Fecha de nacimiento _____
                     Mes   Día   Año

Número de la licencia: _____

Ocupación: _____

Lugar de empleo_____

Estado civil: ☐   Casado (a)
                 ☐   Soltero (a)
                 ☐   Divorciado (a)
                 ☐   Separado (a)
                 ☐   Viudo (a)

Nombre de esposo:_____
_____Primer Nombre_____Segundo Nombre___Apellido Paterno_____Apellido Materno
Nombre de esposa: _____
_____Primer Nombre_____Segundo Nombre___Apellido Paterno_____Apellido Materno/Esposo

En caso de emergencia:_____Teléfono: _____

Firma: _____   Fecha: _____

See back of book for English translation of the basic information form.

44

The Family — La Familia

Putting our families first is something all Americans have in common. This is especially true for Latinos. For them, family values are extremely important. No sacrifice is too great if it helps the family. Children are considered precious gifts. Wives, mothers and grandmothers are also highly respected. Remember that the maternal side of the family is so important that traditional Hispanics carry their mother's surname or *materno apellido* as a part of their complete name. If you have forgotten the four important parts of a Latino's name, please review the chapter called *"Cuál es su nombre completo."*

You are certainly going to hear about members of the family from your Hispanic customers. This topic is something all of us like to talk about!

English	Español	Guide
Aunt	Tía	T-ah
Uncle	Tío	T-oh
Brother	Hermano	air-MAN-oh
Sister	Hermana	air-MAN-ah
Brother-in-law	Cuñado	coon-YA-doe
Sister-in-law	Cuñada	coon-YA-da
Child	Niño *(m)* Niña *(f)*	KNEE-nyo KNEE-nya
Cousin	Primo *(m)* Prima *(f)*	PRE-mo PRE-ma
Daughter	Hija	E-ha
Son	Hijo	E-ho

English	Español	Guide
Daughter-in-law	Nuera	new-**AIR**-rah
Son-in-law	Yerno	**YAIR**-no
Father	Padre	**PA**-dray
Mother	Madre	**MA**-dray
Father-in-law	Suegro	soo-**A**-grow
Mother-in-law	Suegra	soo-**A**-gra
Niece	Sobrina	so-**BREE**-na
Nephew	Sobrino	so-**BREE**-no
Step father	Padrastro	pa-**DRAS**-tro
Step mother	Madrastra	ma-**DRAS**-tra
Step son	Hijastro	e-**HAS**-tro
Step daughter	Hijastra	e-**HAS**-tra
Granddaughter	Nieta	knee-**A**-ta
Grandson	Nieto	knee-**A**-toe
Grandfather	Abuelo	ah-boo-**A**-low
Grandmother	Abuela	ah-boo-**A**-la
Husband	Esposo	es-**POE**-so
Wife	Esposa	es-**POE**-sa

Tips & Tidbits

The Hispanic family is a very close-knit group. The term *familia* extends beyond the nuclear family and includes not only parents and children, but also the entire extended family. In traditional Hispanic families, the father is the "head of the household" and the mother is responsible for the home. Individual family members have a responsibility to aid others in the family when they experience financial problems or a health crisis. You can always depend on your *familia*.

Crimes — Delitos

Because of the way crime statistics have been collected in the past, it's almost impossible to obtain a completely accurate picture of violent offenses within the Hispanic community. Until recently, most data on Hispanic crime has been combined with numbers for Caucasians. In addition, percentages for Black Hispanics have been included with statistics for African-Americans instead of being placed in a separate category. As a result of this inaccurate categorization, crime statistics for both Caucasians and Blacks could be somewhat inflated. It is also possible that data for Hispanics is under-reported. Many years may pass before we are able to gain a true picture of Hispanic crime. Gang violence, cultural assimilation, immigration legislation, drug use, and education about the criminal justice system will all have a bearing on Hispanic crime statistics.

Use the following vocabulary to explain *el problema* to your *suspecho*.

English	Español	Guide
Aggravated assault	Asalto agravado	ah-**SAL**-toe ah-grah-**VA**-doe
Aggravated manslaughter	Homicidio impremeditado agravante	oh-me-**SEE**-d-oh eem-pray-may-d-**TA**-doe ah-grah-**VAHN**-tay
Aggravated sexual assault	Agresión sexual agravante	ah-grey-see-**ON** sex-oo-**AL** ah-grah-**VAHN**-tay
Aggravating factors	Factores agravantes	fac-**TOR**-ace ah-grah-**VAN**-tays

English	Español	Guide
Aid and abet	Ayudar, facilitar e incitar	eye-you-**DAR** fa-see-lee-**TAR** e een-see-**TAR**
Armed robbery	Asalto a mano armada	ah-**SAL**-toe ah **MA**-no are-**MA**-da
Arson	Delito de incendio	day-**LEE**-toe day een-**SEN**-d-oh
Assault	Agresión	ah-grey-see-**ON**
Assault and battery	Asalto con agresión física	ah-**SAL**-toe con ah-grey-see-**ON** **FEE**-see-ca
Bad check	Cheque sin fondos	**CHECK**-kay seen **PHONE**-does
Battery	Agresión física	ah-grey-see-**ON** **FEE**-see-ca
Blackmail	Chantaje	chan-**TA**-hey
Bribe	Soborno	so-**BORN**-no
Burglarize	Escalar para robar	es-ca-**LAR PA**-rah row-**BAR**
Burglary	Escalamiento	es-ca-la-me-N-toe
Capital punishment	Pena de muerte	**PAY**-na day moo-**AIR**-tay
Contributing to the delinquency of a minor	Contribuyendo a la delincuencia de un menor	con-tree-boo-**YEN**-doe al la day-lean-coo-**N**-see-ah day oon may-**NOR**
Counterfeit	Dinero falsificado	d-**NAY**-row fall-see-fee-**CA**-doe
Criminal confinement/kidnapping	Confinamiento criminal	con-fee-na-me-N-toe cree-me-**NAL**
Criminal trespass	Trasgresión criminal	tras-grey-see-**ON** cree-me-**NAL**

English	Español	Guide
Deadly weapon	Arma mortífera	**ARM**-ma mor-**T**-fair-rah
Disorderly conduct	Desorden público	des-**OR**-den **POO**-blee-co
Driving under the influence	Manejando bajo la influencia	ma-nay-**HAN**-doe **BA**-ho la een-flu-**N**-see-ah
Drug possession	Posesión de drogas	po-ses-see-**ON** day **DROW**-gas
Endangering a minor	Arriesgar a un menor	ah-ree-ace-**GAR** ah oon may-**NOR**
Felony	Delito mayor	day-**LEE**-toe ma-**YOUR**
First degree	De primer grado	day pre-**MARE** **GRA**-do
First degree murder	Asesinato en primer grado	ah-say-see-**NA**-toe in pre-**MARE** **GRA**-doe
Fraud	Estafa	es-**TA**-fa
Grand larceny	Hurto mayor	**OOR**-toe ma-**YOUR**
Hit and run	Choque y fuga	**CHO**-kay e **FOO**-ga
Malicious mischief	Travesura maliciosa	trah-ves-**SUE**-rah ma-lee-see-**OH**-sa
Manslaughter	Homicidio involuntario	oh-me-**SEE**-d-oh een-vo-loon-**TA**-ree-oh
Misdemeanor	Delito menor	day-**LEE**-toe may-**NOR**
Murder	Asesinato	ah-ses-see-**NA**-toe
	Homicida	oh-me-**SEE**-da

English	Español	Guide
Offense	Delito	day-LEE-toe
Perjury	Perjurio	pear-WHO-ree-oh
Rape (n)	Violación	v-oh-la-see-ON
Rape (v)	Violar	v-oh-LAR
Rear end accident	Chocar al coche desde atrás	cho-CAR al CO-che DES-day ah-TRAS
Reckless driving	Manejo peligroso	ma-NAY-ho pay-lee-GROSS-so
Sexual assault	Agresión sexual	ah-grey-see-ON sex-oo-AL
Shoplifting	Ratería	rah-ter-REE-ah
Statutory rape	Estupro	es-TOO-pro
Vagrant	Vagabundo	va-ga-BOON-doe
Voluntary manslaughter	Homicidio voluntario	oh-me-SEE-d-oh vo-loon-TA-ree-oh

Tips and Tidbits

Familism in Hispanic families includes both nuclear and extended family. The family is so important that members will often make decisions based on the good of the entire family, rather than for an individual member. Being part of a family network and support group is extremely important, especially for new immigrants. Many US Hispanics continue to practice Catholicism and the divorce rate remains below the national average among first-generation Latinos. However, as Hispanics assimilate into an American society, many of their marriages don't survive. A recent study by the Institute for American Values reported that the marriages of 12% of Mexican immigrant women end in divorce within their first ten years of arriving in the US.

Paperwork and People
Documentos y Personas

Where crime and punishment are concerned, paperwork and people are equally important. Knowing the Spanish vocabulary to make sure your suspect understands his legal rights will require practice and planning. Go slowly and carefully through this list, learning only the words you will use the most at first.

English	Español	Guide
Affidavit	Declaración jurada	day-clar-rah-see-**ON** who-**RAH**-da
Arrest warrant	Demanda de arresto	day-**MAN**-da day ah-**REST**-toe
Attorney	Abogado	ah-bow-**GA**-doe
Clerk	Secretario de la corte	sec-ray-**TAR**-ree-oh day la **CORE**-tay
Court bailiff	Alguacil	al-goo-ah-**SILL**
Defendant	Demandado	day-man-**DA**-do
Defendant in criminal case	Acusado	ah-coo-**SA**-doe
Defense counselor	Abogado defensor *(a)*	ah-bow-**GA**-doe day-fen-**SOAR**
Detective	Detective	day-tec-**T**-vay
Hospital record	Historia clínica	e-**STORE**-ree-ah **CLEE**-knee-ca
Identification	Identificación	e-den-t-fee-ca-see-**ON**
Interpreter	Interprete	een-**TER**-prey-tay
Investigator	Investigador	een-ves-t-ga-**DOOR**
Jury	Jurado	who-**RAH**-doe

English	Español	Guide
Litigant	Litigante	lee-t-**GAN**-tay
Magistrate	Magistrado	ma-hees-**TRA**-doe
Motion	Petición	pay-t-see-**ON**
Order	Orden	**OR**-den
Patrolman	Patrullero	pa-true-**YAIR**-row
Plaintiff	Demandante	day-man-**DAHN**-tay
	Parte acusadora	**PAR**-tay ah-coo-sa-**DOOR**-rah
Police report	Informe policial	een-**FOR**-may po-lee-see-**AL**
Probation officer	Oficial de libertad condicional	oh-fee-see-**AL** day lee-bear-**TAD** con-d-see-on-**NAL**
Restrictive order	Orden de restricción	**OR**-den day ray-strict-see-**ON**
Search warrant	Orden de cateo	**OR**-den day ca-**TAY**-oh
Social security card	Tarjeta de seguridad social	tar-**HEY**-ta day say-goo-ree-**DAD** so-c-**AL**
Translator	Traductor *(a)*	tra-duc-**TOR**
Waiver	Renuncio	ray-**NOON**-see-oh
Waiver of rights form	Documento de renuncia de derechos	doe-coo-**MEN**-toe day ray-**NOON**-see-ah day day-**RAY**-chos
Warrant	Demanda	day-**MAN**-da
Your Honor	Su Señoría	su sen-nor-**REE**-ah

Around the Court House

The court house can be a maze of confusing places. From the basement to the top floor, all of its occupants are bustling. Being able to offer directions to court rooms, the magistrate's office, areas where fees are paid and other basic locations will be important to putting citizens at ease. Use the following lists to give directions to important locations around the court house.

English	Español	Guide
Where is it?	¿Dónde está?	DON-day es-TA
Bath room	Baño	BAHN-yo
	Servicio	ser-V-see-oh
Bench	Estrado	es-TRA-doe
Chambers	Cámara	CA-ma-rah
Court	Juzgado	whose-GA-doe
	Corte	CORE-tay
	Tribunal	tree-boo-NAL
Courthouse	Palacio de justicia	pa-LAS-see-oh day whose-T-see-ah
Courtroom	Sala del tribunal	SA-la del tree-boo-NAL
Hall	Corredor	core-ray-DOOR
Jury room	Sala del jurado	SA-la del who-RAH-doe
Magistrate's Office	Oficina de magistrado	oh-fee-SEEN-na day ma-hees-TRA-doe
Register of Deeds	Registrar de escrituras	ray-hees-TRARE day es-cree-TOO-rahs

English	Español	Guide
Registrar's Office	Oficina de registrado de escrituras	oh-fee-**SEEN**-na day ray-hees-**TRA**-doe day es-cree-**TOO**-rahs
Small Claims Court	Corte de demandas pequeñas	**CORE**-tay day day-**MAN**-das pay-**CANE**-yas
Traffic Court	Corte de tráfico	**CORE**-tay day **TRA**-fee-co
Clerk's Office	Oficina de secretaria	oh-fee-**SEEN**-na day sec-ray-**TAR**-ree-ah

More Directions — Más Direcciones

Combine this list of basic directions with areas of the court house. Now you will be able to offer even more precise directions.

English	Español	Guide
Where is it?	¿Dónde está?	**DON**-day es-**TA**
North	Norte	**NOR**-tay
South	Sur	**SUE**-er
East	Este	**ACE**-tay
West	Oeste	oh-**ACE**-tay
Above	Encima	n-**SEE**-ma
Avenue	Avenida	ah-ven-**KNEE**-da
Behind	Detrás	day-**TRAHS**
Down	Abajo	ah-**BAA**-ho
Here	Aquí	ah-**KEY**
In front of	En frente de	n **FREN**-tay day

English	Español	Guide
Inside	Adentro	ah-**DEN**-tro
Near	Cerca	**CER**-ca
Next to	Al lado de	al **LA**-doe day
Outside	Afuera	ah-foo-**AIR**-ah
Straight ahead	Adelante	ah-day-**LAN**-tay
Street	Calle	**CAI**-yea
There	Allí	ah-**YE**
To the left	A la izquierda	ah la ees-key-**AIR**-dah
Turn	Doble	**DOE**-blay
To the right	A la derecha	ah la day-**RAY**-cha
Up	Arriba	ah-**REE**-ba

Tips and Tidbits

The concept of "personal space", the space in which we feel comfortable in conversation, is a cultural concept. Most North Americans prefer a distance of an arm's length when talking to each another. Hispanics often choose a closer personal space. For most Hispanics, eighteen inches is a comfortable distance.

Around Town

Places around your city or town can provide you with great practice opportunities. The next time you are out on patrol or even running errands when you are off duty, check the list below. *¿A dónde va?* Where are you going? Make a numbered list of the places you intend to go. Using the directions in the previous chapter and places around town allows you to use two important sets of vocabulary at the same time. Group this vocabulary into logical sets. Which places involve travel? Which places involve recreation? Now, let's get going!

English	Español	Guide
Airport	Aeropuerto	ah-eh-row-poo-**AIR**-toe
Bakery	Panadería	pan-ah-day-**REE**-ah
Bank	Banco	**BAN**-co
Barber shop	Peluquería	pay-loo-kay-**REE**-ah
Beauty salon	Salón de belleza	sa-**LAWN** day bay-**YEA**-sa
Church	Iglesia	e-**GLAY**-see-ah
City hall	Municipio	moon-knee-**SEE**-p-oh
Fire department	Departamento de bomberos	day-par-ta-**MEN**-toe day bom-**BAY**-rows
Florist	Florería	floor-ray-**REE**-ah
Gas station	Gasolinera	gas-so-lee-**NAY**-rah
Grocery store	Grosería	gros-eh-**REE**-ah
Hospital	Hospital	os-p-**TAL**
Hotel	Hotel	oh-**TEL**
Jewelry store	Joyería	hoy-eh-**REE**-ah
Laundromat	Lavandería	la-van-day-**REE**-an
Library	Biblioteca	b-lee-oh-**TECK**-ah
Market	Mercado	mare-**CA**-doe
Movie theatre	Cine	**SEEN**-nay
Museum	Museo	moo-**SAY**-oh
Park	Parque	**PAR**-kay
Pharmacy	Farmacia	far-**MA**-see-ah
Police station	Estación de policía	es-ta-see-**ON** day po-lee-**SEE**-ah
Post office	Correo	core-**A**-oh

English	Español	Guide
Restaurant	Restaurante	res-tower-**AHN**-tay
School	Escuela	es-coo-**A**-la
Shoe store	Zapatería	sa-pa-tay-**REE**-ah
Store	Tienda	t-**N**-da
Super market	Super Mercado	soo-**PEAR** mare-**CA**-doe
Theatre	Teatro	tay-**AH**-trow
Train station	Estación de tren	es-ta-see-**ON** day tren
Subway	Metro	**MAY**-tro

Tips and Tidbits

Respecto or respect is an important value in Hispanic culture that is given to an individual based on age or position within the social structure. Senior citizens are granted *respecto* because of their age and life experience. Elders are highly respected in Hispanic families and seniors encourage younger generations to ask questions. Latinos also have a high regard for peers, supervisors and managers who are older than them. In this situation, age is even more important than on-the-job experience. Along with *respecto* go other highly valued traits such as honesty and courage. Members of the medical, legal law enforcement professions also receive *respecto* because of their advanced education and standing within the community. Out of *respecto* for your position, a Hispanic citizen might not want to contradict your opinion. Using your Spanish skills will help you build a trusting relationship with your client so that open communication can take place.

The House — La Casa

It doesn't matter if you are a policeman, firefighter or paramedic, in case of emergency, you could be called upon to search someone's home. This vocabulary will help you get to the right room *pronto!* As you begin to learn the words on this list, think about the rooms in your own home. If you take time to label each room of your house with bilingual sticky notes, you will be able to learn this vocabulary very quickly. Learning Spanish can be easy and fun if you keep the words you are learning right in front of you! When you think you know the Spanish word for a particular room or section of your home, ask a member of your *familia* to scramble the labels. When you can place the correct labels on the right items, you've got your house in order!

English	Español	Guide
Attic	Ático	**AH**-tee-co
Basement	Sótano	**SO**-tan-oh
Bathroom	Baño	**BAN**-yo
Bedroom	Dormitorio	dor-me-**TOR**-e-oh
	Recámara	ray-**CA**-mare-rah
Master bedroom	Dormitorio principal	dor-me-**TOR**-e-oh preen-see-**PAL**
Brick	Ladrillo	la-**DREE**-yo
Cabinet	Gabinete	ga-b-**NAY**-tay
Carpet	Alfombra	al-**FOAM**-bra
Ceiling	Techo	**TAY**-cho
Closet	Armario	are-**MAR**-ree-oh
Den	Estudio	es-**STEW**-dee-oh
Dining room	Comedor	come-a-**DOOR**

English	Español	Guide
Driveway	Camino de entrada	ca-**ME**-no day n-**TRA**-da
Fireplace	Chimenea	che-me-**NAY**-ah
Floor	Piso	**PEE**-so
Garage	Garaje	ga-**RAH**-hey
Hall	Corredor	core-ree-**DOOR**
Kitchen	Cocina	co-**SEE**-nah
Laundry room	Lavandería	la-van-day-**REE**-ah
Living room	Salón	sal-**ON**
Shutter	Contraventana	contra-ven-**TAN**-nah
Pantry	Dispensa	d-**SPEN**-sa
Wall	Pared	par-**RED**
Window	Ventana	ven-**TAN**-nah
Yard	Cesped	**CES**-ped
	Patio	**PA**-tee-oh
	Yarda	yarda

Tips & Tidbits:

Neither the names of businesses nor the names of streets are translated into Spanish. The proper name of your agency represents its brand or trade-mark and should not be translated. Consequently, the name of a street is its proper or given name and should not be translated either. In most Latin American cities, numbers and the words "street" and "avenue" are commonly used in addresses, just as they are in most metropolitan areas of the US.

Instructions — Instrucciones

Listed below are a variety of practical phrases. Because these phrases can be used as commands, they are versatile and *muy importante*. Move them to the top of your practice list.

Here's a tip to remember when using phrases from this list — it's always important to check for comprehension when you begin to use your new Spanish skills. Make sure the Spanish-speaker you are working with understands the instructions you have given. To help with this communication basic, phrase your question this way: *¿Comprende mis instrucciones?* Do you understand my instructions? Remember to <u>always</u> use the word *instructions* rather than *directions*. This could be confusing to some Latinos because the word *dirección* in español can mean *address*. Also, don't forget to add *por favor* or "please" to your *instrucciones*! Courtesy goes a long way towards establishing trust and rapport.

English	Español	Guide
Come here.	Venga aquí.	**VEN**-ga ah-**KEY**.
Let's go.	Vámonos.	**VA**-mo-nos
Go with him.	Vaya con él.	**VA**-ya con **L**
Wait	Espere.	ace-**PEAR**-ray
Stop.	Pare.	**PAR**-ray
Help me.	Ayúdeme.	ay-**U**-day-may
Help him.	Ayúdelo.	ay-**U**-day-low
Like this.	Así.	ah-**SEE**
Not like this.	Así no.	ah-**SEE** no
Show me.	Muéstreme.	moo-**ACE**-tray-may
Good	Bien	b**N**

English	Español	Guide
Point to it	Indíquelo	n-DEE-kay-low
Move that here	Mueve eso aquí	moo-wavy ACE-so ah-KEY
Bring me that	Tráigame eso	try-GA-may ACE-toe
Give it to me	Démelo	DAY-may-low
To the right	A la derecha	a la day-RAY-cha
To the left	A la izquierda	a la ees-kay-AIR-da
Remove these	Quite estos.	KEY-tay ACE-toes
Pick up all these	Recoja todo estos	ray-CO-ha TOE-dos ES-toes
Put it there	Póngalo allí	PON-ga-low ah-YE
Around	Alrededor	al-ray-day-DOOR
Inside	Dentro	DEN-tro
Under	Debajo	day-BA-ho
Carry this.	Lleve esto.	YEA-vay ACE-toe
Open	Abra	AH-bra
Close	Cierre	c-EH-ray
Do it now	Hágalo ahor.	AH-ga-low ah-ORA
Do it later	Hágalo más tarde	AH-ga-low mas TAR-day
Here	Aquí	ah-KEY
There	Allí	ah-YE
A little	Un poco	un PO-ko
A lot	Mucho	MOO-cho

Traffic — Tráfico

Receiving a traffic citation is something that most drivers experience at one time or another. What most Americans don't realize is the process of paying for these tickets or receiving a court date can vary from country to country. Sometimes traffic fines are negotiated at the scene with law enforcement  officials. In some parts of Latin America, **sobornos** *(so-BORN-nos)* or bribes and **mordidas** *(more-DEE-dahs)* or extra fees are used to settle matters on the spot. Also, many countries don't require any type of insurance on vehicles. This can create a huge headache here since it is illegal to drive without liability coverage. In the event of a traffic citation or fender bender, don't be surprised if a Latin American pulls out his wallet to pay you. This isn't a bribe. It's just the way things are done in his country of origin. Many individuals have not had an experience with law enforcement in the US. What a super opportunity to demonstrate "to serve and protect"!

No es legal en los Estados Unidos   *It's not legal in the United States.*
No es lay-GAL in los es-TA-dos oo-KNEE-dos

English	Español	Guide
I am a police officer.	Soy policía.	soy po-lee-SEE-ah
Your name?	¿Su nombre?	sue NOM-bray
I need your license.	Necesito su licencia.	nay-say-SEE-toe sue lee-SEN-see-ah
I need your registration.	Necesito su registro del auto.	nay-say-SEE-toe sue ray-HEES-tro del OW-toe
Do you have identification?	¿Tiene identificación?	t-N-a e-den-t-fee-ca-see-ON

English	Español	Guide
Give it to me, please.	Dámelo, por favor.	DA-may-low pour fa-VOR
Do you have auto insurance?	¿Tiene seguro de vehículo?	t-N-a say-GOO-row day vay-E-coo-low
May I search the car?	¿Puedo registrar el carro?	pooh-A-doe ray-hees-TRAR l CA-row
Where do you live?	¿Dónde vive?	DON-day VEE-vay
Your address, please.	Su dirección, por favor.	sue d-wreck-see-ON, pour fa-VOR
Where do you work?	¿Dónde trabaja?	DON-day tra-BA-ha
Who is your boss?	¿Quién es su jefe?	key-N es sue HEF-ay
Are you drunk?	¿Está borracho?	es-TA bow-RAH-cho
Are you taking drugs?	¿Está tomando drogas?	es-TA toe-MAHN-doe DRO-gas
This is a warning.	Esto es un aviso.	ES-toe es oon ah-V-so
This is a ticket.	Esta es una citación.	es-TA es oona see-ta-see-ON
Your court date is....	Su fecha de corte es....	sue FAY-cha day CORE-tay es
Your tag is expired.	Su placa está vencida.	sue PLA-ca es-TA ven-SEE-da
The inspection is expired.	La inspección está vencida.	la een-spec-see-ON es-TA ven-SEE-da
You don't have a headlight.	No tiene una luz.	no t-N-a oona loose
Do you need help?	¿Necesita ayuda?	nay-say-SEE-ta eye-YOU-da
Do you need a doctor?	¿Necesita un doctor?	nay-say-SEE-ta oon doc-TOR
You were speeding.	Manejaba en exceso de velocidad.	ma-nay-HA-ba in x-SAY-so day vay-low-see-DAD

English	Español	Guide
The speed limit is ...	La limite de velocidades es _____ millas por hora.	la lee-ME-tay day vay-low-see-DA-daces es ____ ME-yas pour OR-rah
You were driving ____ miles per hour.	Manejó ____ millas por hora.	ma-nay-HO ___ ME-yas pour OR-rah

You're Under Arrest — ¡Está Arestado!

In tense situations, it is easy to become nervous, especially when you are using new language skills. For this scenario, it's best to practice often. If it's feasible, practice the phrases in this chapter with your partner as often as possible. Start slowly and learn only a few phrases each week. To prioritize this vocabulary, think critically about what you say when you make an arrest. Then make a list of those phrases or highlight the ones you use from the list below.

English	Español	Guide
Calm down	Cálmese	CAL-may-say
Close the door with your foot!	¡Cierra la puerta con su pie!	see-AIR-rah la poo-AIR-ta con sue p-AY
Cut the ignition off!	¡Apague el carro!	ah-PA-gay l CA-row
Describe it.	Descríbalo.	des-CREE-ba-low
Driver	Chofer	cho-FAIR
Drop the keys!	¡Suelte las llaves!	sue-L-tay las YA-vays
Face down on the ground!	¡Boca abajo!	BOW-ca ah-BA-ho

English	Español	Guide
Get back in the car!	¡Regrese al carro!	ray-**GREY**-say al **CA**-row
Get out of the car!	¡Salga del carro!	**SAL**-ga del **CA**-row
Hands here!	¡Manos aquí!	**MA**-nos ah-**KEY**
Hands outside the car!	¡Manos fuera del carro!	**MA**-nos foo-**AIR**-rah del **CA**-row
Hands up!	¡Manos arriba!	**MA**-nos ah-**REE**-ba
Keep your hands behind your neck.	Mantenga las manos detrás del cuello.	man-**TEN**-ga las **MA**-nose day-**TRAS** del coo-**WAY**-yo
Kneel down!	¡Arrodíllese!	ah-row-**D**-yea-say
Look at me.	¡Mírame!	**ME**-rah-may
Lower the music.	¡Baje la música!	**BA**-hey la **MOO**-see-ca
Lower the window!	¡Baje la ventana!	**BA**-hey la ven-**TAHN**-na
Move very slowly.	Muévase muy despacio.	moo-**WAY**-vay-say mooy des-**PA**-see-oh
Open the door from outside!	¡Abra la puerta de afuera!	**AH**-bra la poo-**AIR**-ta day ah-foo-**AIR**-rah
Passenger	Pasajero	pa-sa-**HAIR**-row
Passenger behind	Pasajero detrás	pa-sa-**HAIR**-row day-**TRAS**
Passenger in front	Pasajero enfrente	pa-sa-**HAIR**-row in **FREN**-tay
Put your weapon on the ground.	Ponga el arma en el suelo.	**PONG**-ga l **ARM**-ma in l sue-**A**-low
Raise your shirt!	¡Levántese su camisa!	lay-**VAN**-ta-say sue ca-**ME**-sa
Sit down!	¡Siéntese!	see-**N**-tay-say
Slowly!	¡Despacio!	des-**PA**-see-oh

English	Español	Guide
Stay there!	¡Quédese allí!	**KAY**-day-say ah-**YE**
Stop!	¡Párese!	**PA**-ray-say
Stop or I'll shoot!	Párese o disparo	**PA**-ray-say oh dees-**PA**-row
Take out the keys!	¡Saque las llaves!	**SA**-kay las **YA**-vays
Turn around!	¡Dése vuelta!	**DAY**-say voo-**L**-ta
Walk backwards!	¡Camine hacía atrás!	ca-**ME**-nay ah-**SEE**-ah ah-**TRAS**
You're under arrest!	¡Está arrestado!	es-**TA** ah-res-**TA**-doe

Miranda Rights

Reading Miranda Rights to a Spanish-speaking suspect can be challenging for many reasons. Although language is the first obstacle to the suspect and the officer, it is not the only one. While many police departments provide a translated version of the Miranda Rights, many Hispanics are unable to read this document. According to the 2000 US Census, almost one-third of Hispanics over the age of 27 are functionally illiterate. This inability compounds the problem of understanding the most critical element of the procedure. Secondly, people being read their Miranda Rights often do not comprehend these rights even though they understand the words. For many individuals, these rights are completely foreign because nothing like them exists in their country of origin. In addition, fear of law enforcement is pervasive in Hispanic culture. Why? In many countries no distinction exists between the police and the military. This basic cultural difference can lead to serious misunderstandings.

English	Español	Guide
You have the right to remain silent.	Tiene el derecho a guardar silencio.	t-N-a l day-RAY-cho ah goo-are-DAR see-LEN-see-oh
Anything you say can be and may be used against you in a court of law.	Lo que diga puede ser usada en su contra en una corte de ley.	low kay D-ga poo-A-day ser oo-SA-da in sue CON-tra in OO-na CORE-tay day lay
You have the right to speak to a lawyer and to have a lawyer present while you are being questioned.	Tiene el derecho a un abogado y de tenerlo presente durante interrogación.	t-N-a l day-RAY-cho ah oon ah-bow-GA-doe e day ten-NAIR-low pray-SEN-tay do-RAHN-tay een-ter-row-ga-see-ON
If you want a lawyer before or during questioning but cannot afford to hire a lawyer, one will be appointed to represent you at no cost before any questioning.	Si no tiene dinero para conseguir un abogado, uno le será designado antes de cualquier pregunta, si usted desea.	see no t-N-a d-NAY-row PA-rah con-say-GEAR oon ah-bow-GA-doe OO-no lay say-RAH day-seeg-NA-doe AHN-tays day coo-all-key-AIR pray-GOON-ta see oo-STED day-SAY-ah
Do you understand each of these rights I have explained to you?	¿Comprende usted cada uno de los derechos que yo le he explicado?	com-PREN-day oo-STED CA-da OO-no day los day-RAY-chos kay yo lay ay x-plea-CA-doe

English	Español	Guide
Having these rights in mind, do you now wish to answer questions?	¿Con estos derechos en mente, quiere contestar las preguntas ahora?	con **ES**-toes day-**RAY**-chos in **MEN**-tay key-**AIR**-ray con-tes-**TAR** las pray-**GOON**-tas ah-**OR**-ah
Do you now wish to answer questions without a lawyer present?	¿Quiere contestar las preguntas sin la presencia de un abogado?	key-**AIR**-ray con-tes-**TAR** las pray-**GOON**-tas seen la pray-**SEN**-see-ah day oon a h-bow-**GA**-doe

Under the Influence — Baja la Influencia

In 2000, *the Annals of Emergency Medicine* published a report stating that Hispanics are 75% more likely to die in an automobile accident than non-Hispanic Caucasians. Alarmingly, the study also found that Latinos are twice as likely to drive under the influence of alcohol. The study revealed that Hispanics believe it requires the consumption of four to six alcoholic beverages before a driver becomes intoxicated. This assumption can lead to shocking consequences when family members are along for the ride! The census figures confirm the Hispanic population to be both the youngest and fastest-growing segment in America. This rapid growth combined with a higher tendency to drive after drinking or to ride with an impaired driver is a recipe for disaster.

**Note: DWI laws vary from state to state. Read the statements in the following table carefully to make sure that they are applicable in your area.

You have been charged with operating a vehicle upon a highway or public vehicular area while committing an implied consent offense. You will be requested to submit to a chemical analysis to determine your alcohol concentration. It is first required that you are informed both verbally and in writing of your rights which are as follows:

Usted está acusado de manejar un vehículo por un camino o área para vehículos mientras cometía una ofensa de consentimiento implicado, esto quiere decir que si usted se niega a hacerse la prueba de soplar en el intoxicó metro, el estado puede revocar su privilegio de manejar un vehículo de motor por un año. Se le pedirá que se someta a un análisis químico para determinar la cantidad de alcohol que usted tiene en su cuerpo. Es preciso informarle en forma oral y también en forma escrita de sus derechos que son los siguientes:

English	Español
You have the right to refuse to be tested.	Usted tiene el derecho a negarse a hacerse la prueba.
Refusal to take any required test or tests will result in an immediate revocation of your driving privilege for at least 30 days and an additional 12-month revocation by the Division of Motor Vehicles.	El negarse a hacerse la prueba o pruebas que se le pidan resultará en la revocación inmediata de su privilegio de manejar por un mínimo de treinta días y otra revocación de doce meses por parte de la División de vehículos de motor.
The test results, or the fact of your refusal, will be admissible in evidence at trial for the offense charged.	Los resultados de la prueba o la acción de negarse a hacerse la prueba pueden ser usados como evidencia en su contra en el juicio por la ofensa de la que se le acusa.

English	Español
Your driving privilege will be revoked immediately for at least 30 days if:	Su privilegio de manejar será revocado inmediatamente por treinta días si:
The test reveals an alcohol concentration of 0.08 or more, or	La prueba indica que usted tiene una concentración de alcohol en su cuerpo de 0.08 o más, o
You were driving a commercial motor vehicle and the test reveals an alcohol concentration of 0.04 or more.	Estaba manejando un vehículo de motor comercial y la prueba indica un resultado de 0.04 o más.
You are under 21 years of age and the test reveals any alcohol concentration.	Usted tiene menos de veintiuno años y la prueba indica cualquier concentración de alcohol en su cuerpo.
You may have a qualified person of your own choosing administer a chemical test or tests in addition to any test administered at the direction of the charging officer.	Usted tiene el derecho a escoger a una persona calificada para que le administre las pruebas químicas necesarias además de aquellas que se le administren por orden del oficial que le acusa.
You have the right to call an attorney and select a witness to view for you the testing procedures, but the testing may not be delayed for these purposes longer than 30 minutes from the time you are notified of your rights.	Usted tiene el derecho de llamar a un abogado y de escoger a un testigo para que observe los procedimientos de la prueba, sin embargo, la prueba no se puede retrasar por más de treinta minutos para que usted llame a estas personas. Estos treinta minutos se comienzan a contra desde el momento que usted se le notifica sus derechos.
Do you want a lawyer or a witness?	¿Quiere usted a un abogado o a un testigo?
Do you wish to call anyone?	¿Quiere llamar a alguien?

Signs — Letreros

Working a license check or moving drivers safely through a construction zone can be dangerous work. You never know what is going to happen. Most highway signs are similar from country to country throughout the Americas. However, it's still a great idea to know phrases for the basic signs and be able to give instructions if you are working on any sort of traffic detail. The following *lista* will help you to give the appropriate *instrucciones* in almost any *situación*.

English	Español	Guide
Closed	Cerrado	ser-**RAH**-doe
Curve	Curva	**COOR**-va
Detour	Desviación	des-v-ah-see-**ON**
Do not enter	Prohibido Entrar	pro-**E**-b-doe n-**TRARE**
Do not litter	No tirar basura	no tear-**RAHARE**
Do not pass	Prohibido pasar	pro-**E**-b-doe pa-**CZAR**
Don't walk	No caminar	no ca-me-**NAR**
Emergency	Emergencia	a-mare-**HEN**-see-ah
Entrance	Entrada	n-**TRA**-da
Exit	Salida	sa-**LEE**-da
Handicapped	Minusválidos	me-noose-**VA**-lee-dose
Narrow road	Camino estrecho	ca-**ME**-no es-**TRAY**-cho
No "U" turn	Prohibida la vuelta en "U"	pro-**E**-b-da la voo-**L**-ta en **OO**

English	Español	Guide
No left turn	No doblar a la izquierda	no doe-**BLAR** ah la ees-key-**AIR**-da
No parking	Estacionamiento prohibido	es-ta-see-oh-na-me-**N**-toe pro-**E**-b-doe
	No parque	no **PAR**-kay
	No estacionar	no es-ta-see-on-**NAR**
No smoking	No fumar	no **FOO**-mar
One way	Dirección única	d-wreck-see-**ON** **OO**-knee-ca
Open	Abierto	ah-b-**AIR**-toe
Out of order	Descompuesto	des-com-poo-**ACE**-toe
Passing lane	Pista para pasar	**PEES**-ta **PA**-rah pa-**CZAR**
Railroad crossing	Cruce de ferrocarril	**CRUZ**-say day fay-row-ca-**REEL**
Restrooms	Servicios	ser-**V**-see-ohs
	Servicios sanitarios	ser-**V**-see-ohs sahn-knee-**TAR**-ree-ohs
	Baños	**BAN**-yos
Road closed	Camino cerrado	ca-**ME**-no ser-**RAH**-doe
Road crossing	Cruce de caminos	**CRUZ**-say day ca-**ME**-nos
School zone	Zona escolar	**SEW**-na es-co-**LAR**
Slow	Despacio	des-**PA**-see-oh

English	Español	Guide
Speed limit	Velocidad Máxima	vay-low-see-DAD MAX-e-ma
Stop	Parada Alto	pa-RAH-da AL-toe
Stop ahead	Parada próxima	pa-RAH-da PROX-see-ma
Traffic circle	Glorieta	glor-ree-EH-ta
Wait	Espere	es-PEAR-ray
Walk	Camine	ca-ME-nay
Wrong way	Vía equivocada	V-ah a-key-vo-CA-da
Yield	Ceda el paso	SAY-da l PA-so

Domestic Violence — Violencia Doméstica

Culturally, one of the most important things in Latin American life is *la familia.* Families spend as much time as possible together, and they are very close-knit. Family members depend heavily on each other and support each other, no matter where they are. The family is so important that personal decisions are often based on the needs of the entire family, rather than the needs of one individual.

For many Hispanics in the US, domestic abuse is on the rise, despite centering cultural values on families and children. Sadly, according to a recent study at the University of South Carolina, 70 percent of Hispanic women surveyed reported they were victims of domestic violence. Nationwide surveys also reveal that Hispanic women are more likely to be victims of domestic abuse than other nationalities. A common tactic used by abusers is to isolate their victims. For Latin American women who speak only

Spanish and work inside the home, this is easy to do. Their isolation is intensified by the fact that their families may live in other countries far away from them. These women have no network of help and support which puts them at an even greater risk.

Hispanic culture places great value in maintaining the family's integrity and reputation. While this is a wonderful cultural value, a Hispanic female victim of domestic violence may not seek help because she fears it will bring shame upon her family. The guilt felt by many women often prevents them from seeking help. To further complicate the issue, studies also indicate that many Hispanic victims are unaware that resources exist to help them escape and rebuild their lives.

In volatile situations such as these, use the following questions to obtain more information *¿Qué pasó?* (What happened?). Most of these important questions are designed to give you a *sí* or *no* response.

English	Español	Guide
How many people are here?	¿Cuántas personas están aquí?	coo-**WAN**-tas pear-**SEWN**-nas es-**TAHN** ah-**KEY**
Are there any children here?	¿Hay niños aquí?	eye **NEEN**-yos ah-**KEY**
Are there any weapons?	¿Hay armas?	eye **ARM**-as
Where are they?	¿Dónde están?	**DON**-day es-**TAHN**
Show me.	Muéstreme.	moo-**ES**-tray-may
Are there any drugs in the house?	¿Hay drogas en la casa?	eye **DRO**-gas in la **CA**-sa
Was he/she drinking?	¿Estuvo tomando alcohol?	es-**TOO**-vo to-**MAHN**-doe al-co-**HALL**
Does he/she take drugs?	¿Toma drogas?	**TOE**-ma **DRO**-gas

English	Español	Guide
Does he/she have a history of mental illness?	¿Tiene una historia de enfermedad mental?	t-N-a OO-na ees-STORE-ree-ah day in-fer-me-DAD men-TAL
Are you hurt?	¿Está herido?	es-TA air-REE-doe
Do you need a doctor?	¿Necesita un doctor?	nay-say-SEE-ta oon doc-TOR
Where does it hurt?	¿Dónde le duele?	DON-day lay do-A-lay
Did he hit your children?	¿Les pegó a sus niños?	lace pay-GO ah seus NEEN-yos
Do you want to press charges?	¿Quiere acusarle a su esposo?	key-AIR-ray ah-coo-SAR ah sue es-POE-so
You need to see the magistrate.	Necesita visitar al magistro.	nay-say-SEE-ta v-see-TAR al ma-HEES-tro

Tips & Tidbits

1. According to the National Institute of Health, intimate partner violence (IPV) is a major public health problem in the US. 17% of Hispanic couples who were surveyed reported an incident of male-to-female partner violence in the 12 months preceding the survey.

2. Risk factors for IPV are strongly related to socioeconomic factors such as alcohol abuse. Domestic violence is both a national and worldwide crisis. According to a 2000 UNICEF study, 20-50% of the entire female population will become victims of domestic violence.

3. The Department of Justice reports that Hispanics become victims of overall violence at a higher rate than non-Hispanics.

The Dispatcher — El Expedidor

Look carefully at the two words in this chapter title. These two words have a very strong relationship. Does the Spanish word remind you of the English word "expedite"? In English, when we expedite a package or a message, we want to get it out as quickly as possible — and that's exactly what you are doing if you work at a 911 call center! In your important position, time and efficiency are critical. We suggest that you take this page from your manual and keep it handy at your desk. Practice often!

English	Español	Guide
911 Emergency	Nueve uno uno emergencia	new-**WAVE**-a **OO**-no **OO**-no a-mare-**HEN**-see-ah
I'm the dispatcher.	Soy el expedidor.	soy l x-pay-d-**DOOR**
	Soy la expedidora.*(f)*	soy la x-pay-d-**DOOR**-rah
What's the problem?	¿Cuál es el problema?	coo-**ALL** ace el probe-**LAY**-ma
Do you speak English?	¿Habla inglés?	**AH**-bla eng-**LACE**
Can anyone there speak English?	¿Hay alguien allá que puede hablar inglés?	eye al-gee-N eye-**YA** kay poo-**A**-day ah-**BLAR** eng-**LACE**
This is not an emergency.	Este no es una emergencia.	**ACE**-tay no ace **OO**-na a-mare-**HEN**-see-ah
Please call the police at *(Insert your office number)*	Favor de llamar el policía a	fa-**VOR** day ya-**MAR** el po-lee-**SEE**-ah ah

English	Español	Guide
What is your complete name?	¿Cuál es su nombre completo?	coo-**ALL** es sue **NOM**-bray com-**PLAY**-toe
What is your address?	¿Cuál es su dirección?	coo-**ALL** es sue d-wreck-see-**ON**
Do you live at this address?	¿Vive a esta dirección?	**VEE**-vay ah **ACE**-ta d-wreck-see-**ON**
In what apartment?	¿En qué apartamento?	en kay ah-par-ta-**MEN**-toe
In what building?	¿En qué edificio?	en kay a-dee-**FEE**-see-oh
What is your date of birth?	¿Cuál es su fecha de nacimiento?	coo-**ALL** ace sue **FAY**-cha day Na-see-me-**N**-toe
Is someone sick?	¿Alguien está enfermo?	al-gee-**N** ace-**TA** n-**FAIR**-mo
Is he/she breathing?	¿Respire?	ray-**SPEAR**-a
Is someone missing?	¿Alguien está desaparecido?	al-gee-**N** ace-**TA** des-ah-par-a-**SEE**-doe
Daughter	Hija	**EE**-ha
Son	Hijo	**EE**-ho
Husband	Esposo	es-**PO**-so
Wife	Esposa	es-**PO**-sa
Baby	Bebe	bay-**BAY**
Who is hurt?	¿Quién se duele?	key-**N** say doo-**A**-lay
Who hurt you?	¿Quién le dolió?	key-**N** lay doe-lee-**OH**
Ambulance	Ambulancia	am-boo-**LAN**-see-ah
Fire department	Bomberos	bomb-**BAY**-rows
Hospital	Hospital	os-pee-**TAL**

English	Español	Guide
Gun	Pistola	pees-**TOE**-la
Knife	Cuchillo	coo-**CHEE**-yo
Get everyone out of the house now.	Favor de evacuar la casa ahora.	fa-**VOR** day a-va-coo-**ARE** la **KA**-sa ah-**OR**-ah
Quickly	Pronto	**PRON**-toe
Laceration/cut	Herida	hair-**REE**-da
Bleeding	Hemorragia	a-more-**RAH**-he-ah
Stay where you are.	Permanezca donde usted está.	pear-ma-**NAYS**-ka **DON**-day oo-**STED** ace-**TA**
The police are coming.	La policía viene.	la po-lee-**SEE**-ah vee-**N**-nay
The fire department is coming.	Los bomberos vienen.	los bomb-**BAY**-rows vee-**N**-en
The ambulance is coming.	La ambulancia viene.	la am-boo-**LANCE**-see-ah vee-**N**-nay
What direction did he leave in?	¿En qué dirección salió él?	en kay d-wreck-see-**ON** sa-lee-**OH** el
What direction did she leave in?	¿En qué dirección salió ella?	en kay d-wreck-see-**ON** sa-lee-**OH** A-ya
What direction did they leave in?	¿En qué dirección salieron ellos?	N kay d-wreck-see-**ON** sa-lee-**AIR**-ron A-yos

Tips & Tidbits

With Hispanics, communication is characterized by *respeto* (respect). Their interactions contain an element of formality, especially when older persons are involved. Over-familiarity such as the touch of a stranger or the casual use of a person's first name is not appreciated early in the relationship.

Drugs — Drogas

Drug addition is a complicated illness involving social, cultural, psychological and biological factors. Research on drug use in the Hispanic community is just beginning to include sufficient data for serious study. According to the National Hispanic Science Network on Drug Abuse, rates for illicit drug use and dependence are highest for Hispanics (7.8%), followed by Caucasians (7.5%) and African-Americans (6.2%).

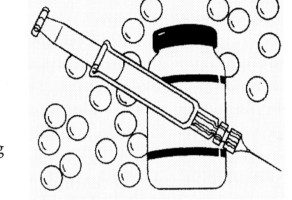

One goal of NHSN is to provide research that will help determine how traditional cultural values and acculturation play a role in Hispanic drug misuse. A disturbing trend reveals more drug use and abuse in US-born Latinos than in immigrants. Studies also indicate that higher levels of acculturation into American society lead to more drug use.

Why is drug use higher in Latinos with a greater level of acculturation?

You would think that a higher level of cultural adaptation would result in greater access to drug education and services. However, this presumption is a misconception. Hispanics report as much need for drug counseling and intervention as other groups. Sadly, they are more likely to report that services are inaccessible to them. When they do receive services, Hispanics are also less likely to be satisfied with them. This dissatisfaction is largely due to our system's lack of Spanish-speaking healthcare workers and counselors who can provide the necessary level of customer service. In addition to language barriers, cultural misconnections are prevalent. A Hispanic who seeks drug treatment under these conditions may feel alienated which complicates and delays recovery. Perhaps the stress of trying to "fit in" to American society, increased income gained from better economic opportunities, and changing ingrained traditional values all provide enough stressors for increased drug abuse and addiction.

As you interact with Hispanic teens in schools and other places, you may have an opportunity to provide guidance and leadership on the subject of drug use. Review the list of common street drugs below. Notice that many of the words in this vocabulary list are similar to their English translations. Slang also plays an important role in drug-related conversation. There are no cultural differences with the use of slang on this subject! These terms can vary from one part of the country to another and between different Hispanic cultures. However, because of the similarities in the words, your communication will still be very effective. In situations where illegal drug use is suspected, using *Spanglish* can also be a real asset. For your convenience, several *Spanglish* terms for common substances are listed under the more conventional term for the drug listed.

English	Español	Guide
Alcohol	Alcohol	al-co-**HOL**
Amphetamine	Anfetamina	ahn-fet-ta-**ME**-na
	Rosa	**ROW**-sa
Barbiturate	Barbitúrico	bar-b-**TOO**-ree-co
Cannabis	Cannabis	can-na-**BEES**
Cocaine	Cocaína	co-kay-**E**-na
	Mujer	moo-**HAIR**
	Yeyo	**YEA**-yo
	Cápsula	**CAP**-sue-la
Cocaine	Coca	**CO**-ca
	Dama blanca	**DA**-ma **BLAN**-ca
	Mujer blanca	moo-**HAIR BLAN**-ca

English	Español	Guide
	Nieve	knee-A-vay
	Perico	peh-**REE**-co
	Polvo	**POLE**-vo
	Talco	**TAL**-co
Cocaine and marijuana mixed	Basuco	ba-**SUE**-co
Cocaine and tobacco	Monos	**MO**-nose
Crack cocaine	El crack	l crack
	Patico	pa-**T**-co
	Piedras	p-**A**-dras
	Roca	**ROW**-ca
Crack cocaine and marijuana	Diablito	d-ah-**BLEE**-toe
	Duros	**DO**-rows
Crack cocaine user	Pipero	p-**PAY**-row
Dealer	Perlas	**PEAR**-las
Depressants	Sedantes	say-**DAHN**-tays
Dexedrine	Dextro anfetamina	**DEX**-tro ahn-fet-ta-**ME**-na
Hallucinogens	Alucinógenos	ah-lou-seen-**OH**-hen-cos
Hashish	Hachís	ah-**CHEES**
Heroin	Heroína	hair-row-**EEN**-na
	Caballo	ca-**BA**-yo

English	Español	Guide
	Caballo blanco	ca-**BA**-yo **BLAN**-co
	Diablito	d-ah-**BLEE**-toe
	Bonita	bow-**KNEE**-ta
	Brea	**BRAY**-ah
	Carga	**CAR**-ga
	Carne	**CAR**-nay
	Chapopote	cha-po-**PO**-tay
	Chatarra	cha-**TAR**-rah
	Chicle	**CHI**-clay
	Chiva	**CHI**-va
	Cocofan (brown tar heroin)	co-co-**FAN**
	Goma (black tar heroin)	**GO**-ma
	Gato	**GA**-toe
	Hombre	**OM**-bray
	Manteca	man-**TAY**-ca
	Tecata	tay-**CA**-ta

English	Español	Guide
	Tigre	T-grey
	Tigre blanco	T-grey **BLAN**-co
	Tigre del norte	T-grey del **NOR**-tay
	Vidrio	**V**-dree-oh
	Zoquete	so-**KAY**-tay
Joint	Leno	**LAY**-no
	Pito	**P**-toe
LSD	LDS	l-ay day s-ay
	Ácido	**AH**-see-doe
Marijuana	Marihuana	ma-re-**WHO**-ah-na
	Hierba	e-**AIR**-ba
	Pasto	**PAS**-toe
	Cartucho	car-**TOO**-cho
	Coliflor tostao	co-lee-**FLOR** toes-**TA**-oh
	Cosa	**CO**-sa
	Doña Juana	**DON**-ya **WHO**-ah-na
	Mota	**MO**-ta
	Juan Valdez	who-**AN** val-**DEZ**

English	Español	Guide
	Juanita	wha-**KNEE**-ta
	Loco	**LOW**-co
	Mafu	**MA**-foo
	Grifa	**GREE**-fa
	Marimba	ma-**REAM**-ba
	Rubia	**ROO**-b-ah
	Santa María	**SAN**-ta ma-**REE**-ah
	Sastras	**SAS**-tras
	Sinse	**SEEN**-say
Methamphetamine	Metanfetamina	met-ahn-fete-ah-**ME**-na
	Meth	meth
	Hielo	ee-**A**-low
	Bombita	bom-**B**-ta
	Cristal	chris-**TAL**
	Cristina	**chris-TEE**-na
Morphine	Morfina	mor-**FEE**-na
Mushrooms	Psilocybina	see-low-see-**B**-na
	Hombrecitos	om-bray-**SEE**-toes

English	Español	Guide
	Mujercitos	moo-hair-SEE-toes
Narcotics	Narcóticos	nar-CO-t-cos
Opium	Opio	OH-p-oh
	Cruz	Cruz
	Mira	ME-rah
PCP	Polvo de ángel	POLE-vo day AN-hel
	Niebla	knee-A-blah
	Paz	pas
	Polvo de estrellas	POLE-vo day es-TRAY-yas
PCP and marijuana	Yerba mala	YER-ba MA-la
	Fríos	FREE-ohs
Peyote	Peyote	pay-OH-tay
Rohypnol	La buena	la boo-WAYNA-na
Sedative	Sedante	say-DAHN-tay
Stimulants	Estimulantes	es-steam-oo-LAHN-tays
Tranquilizer	Tranquilizante	tran-key-lee-ZAHN-tay

Tips and Techniques

The brain seems to process body language signals faster than words. Using body language and crisp hand signals when you speak Spanish will give you an advantage. Use body language to reinforce your words for maximum effectiveness.

Weapons — Armas

No doubt, you will come into contact with all sorts of offenses and the weapons used to perpetrate them. Violent crimes can be committed with so many different objects. Take note of this list which contains an assortment of common weapons.

English	Español	Guide
Ammunition	Munición	moo-knee-see-**ON**
Baseball bat	Palo de béisbol	**PA**-low day **BAY**-ees-bowl
Belt	Cinturón	seen-to-**ROAN**
Billy club	Garrote	ga-**ROW**-tay
Bomb	Bomba	**BOMB**-ba
Bottle	Botella	bow-**TAY**-ya
Brass knuckles	Manoplas	ma-**NO**-plas
Brick	Ladrillo	la-**DREE**-yo
Bullet	Bala	**BA**-la
Caliber	Calibre	ca-**LEE**-bray
Chain	Cadena	ca-**DAY**-na
Club	Palo	**PA**-low
Concealed weapon	Arma de fuego escondida	**ARE**-ma day foo-**WAY**-go es-con-**D**-da
Dagger	Daga	**DA**-ga
Dynamite	Dinamita	d-na-**ME**-ta
Explosive	Explosivo	x-plo-**SEE**-vo

English	Español	Guide
Firearms	Arma de fuego	**ARE**-ma day foo-**WAY**-go
Grenade	Granada	gra-**NA**-da
Hammer	Martillo	mar-**T**-yo
Hatchet	Hacha	**AH**-cha
Knife (Shiv)	Cuchillo	coo-**CHEE**-yo
Machine gun	Ametralladora	ah-may-tra-ya-**DOOR**-rah
Nunchuk sticks	Chacos	cha-**COS**
Pistol (Hand gun)	Pistola	pees-**TOE**-la
Razor	Navaja barbera	na-**VA**-ha bar-**BEAR**-rah
Revolver	Revólver	ray-**VOL**-vair
Rifle	Rifle	**REEF**-lay
	Fusil	foo-**SEAL**
Rock	Roca	**ROW**-ca
Rounds	Tiros	**T**-rows
Shell casing	Cartucho	car-**TOO**-cho
Shotgun	Escopeta	es-co-**PET**-ta
Shotgun (Double-barreled)	Escopeta de dos cañones	es-co-**PET**-ta day dose can-**YOWN**-ace
Silencer	Silenciador	see-len-see-ah-**DOOR**
Snub-nosed revolver	Revolver de cañón corto	ray-**VOL**-vair day can-**YON** **CORE**-toe

English	Español	Guide
Switchblade	Navaja automática	na-**VA**-ha ow-toe-**MA**-tee-ca
Tire iron	Quitallantas	key-ta-**YAN**-nas
Whip	Látigo	**LA**-tee-go
Wire	Alambre	ah-**LAM**-bray

Profanity — Maldiciones

These phrases are included only because you might hear them in tense situations. Knowing them could save the life of you or your partner. We do not recommend you use these phrases in everyday conversation! In many cases, they are inflammatory and could make a bad *situación* much worse!

English	Español	Guide
Ass	Culo	**COO**-low
	Fundillo	foon-**D**-yo
Asshole!	Pendejo	pen-**DAY**-ho
Balls	Huevos	who-**WAVE**-ohs
	Albóndigas	al-**BON**-d-gas
	Cojones	co-**HONE**-ace
Beat the shit out of him!	¡Dále una pateadura!	**DA**-lay **OO**-na pa-tay-**DOO**-rah
Blast him!	Fogonéalo!	foe-gone-**A**-ah-low
Blast him!	¡Dispárale un trancazo!	eees-**PA**-rah-lay oon tran-**CA**-so

English	Español	Guide
Blow his head off!	Vuélale la cabeza!	voo-A-la-lay la ca-BAY-sa
Damn it!	Carajo	ca-RAH-ho
Damn!	Pinche	PEEN-chay
	Coño	CONE-yo
	Maldita sea	mal-D-ta SAY-ah
Devil	Diablo	d-AH-blow
Drooling idiot!	¡Baboso!	ba-BOW-so
Fuck him up!	¡Chíngalo!	CHING-ga-low
Fuck yourself!	¡Vete a la chingada!	VAY-tay ah la ching-GA-da
Gay	Maricón	ma-ring-CON
	Hueco	who-A-co
	Mariposa	ma-ree-PO-sa
Get him out of the way!	¡Llévatelo por delante!	YEA-va-tay-low pour day-LAN-tay
Go fuck your mother.	¡Chinga a tu madre!	CHING-ga ah to MA-dray
Go to hell.	¡Va al infiero!	va al enn-fee-A-row
I shit in your mother's milk.	¡Me cago en la leche de tu madre!	may CA-go in la LAY-chay day to MA-dray
Keep him busy! Get rid of him!	¡Mándalo a pasear!	MAN-da-low ah pa-say-ARE
Kick him!	¡Patéalo!	pa-TAY-ah-low
Kill him!	¡Mátalo!	MA-ta-low
Kiss my ass!	¡Bésame culo!	BAY-sa-may COO-low

English	Español	Guide
Lesbian	Monflora	mon-**FLOOR**-rah
Motherfucker	Mal nacido	mal na-**SEE**-doe
Penis	Bicho	**B**-cho
	Pistola	pees-**TOE**-la
Prick	Cabrón	ca-**BRON**
Punk	Escuincle	es-coo-**INK**-lay
Shit	Mierda	me-**AIR**-da
Shove it up your ass!	¡Métetelo en fundío!	**MAY**-tay-tay-low in foon-**D**-oh
Son of a bitch.	Hijo de puta	E-ho day **POO**-ta
Stab him!	¡Pícalo!	**P**-ca-low
Stupid	Güey	goo-**WAY**
Whore	Puta	**POO**-ta

Firefighters — Bomberos

In your profession, quick responses and even quicker thinking are essential. No one knows more than you that every second counts! Just as running drills with equipment to cut response time is crucial, running language drills can be just as effective. When you are learning a new language, you will naturally be nervous. Sometimes the nervousness and rush of adrenaline that goes with this process will make you feel like you can't remember anything you've studied. Practicing as often as you can and visualizing what people say in different situations will help you to overcome this anxiety. Try to practice a different situation every three days. On the first day, determine what your scenario will be and gather your phrases.

Run your drill several times on the second day. Follow up on the third day by rethinking the phrases you included in your drill. If you missed something, make sure to add it to your notes. Keep adding and revising your notes each time you practice. Every time you use your Spanish on the job, add that information to your records as well.

Here are key phrases you should practice as often as possible. In addition to these phrases, use body language to help you make your point. The brain processes gestures faster than it does words. Body language is an extremely important part of the communication process.

English	Español	Guide
Fire	Fuego	foo-A-go
How did the fire start?	¿Cómo comenzó el fuego?	CO-mo co-men-SO l foo-A-go
Where	¿Dónde?	DON-day
When did the fire start?	¿Cuándo comenzó el fuego?	coo-AN-doe co-men-SO l foo-A-go
Who started the fire?	¿Quién comenzó el fuego?	Key-N co-men-SO L Foo-A-go
Who called the firemen?	¿Quién llamó a los bomberos?	Key-N ya-MO ah los Bom-BAY-rows
What time?	¿A qué hora?	Ah kay HOR-rah
Are you hurt?	¿Está usted herida?	ace-TA oo-STED air-REE-da
Are you in pain?	¿Tiene dolor?	t-N-ay doe-LORE
Where?	¿Dónde?	DON-day
Are you burned?	¿Se quemó?	say kay-MO

English	Español	Guide
Are others inside?	¿Hay otros adentro?	eye **OH**-tros ah-**DEN**-tro
How many	¿Cuántos?	coo-**AN**-toes
Are pets inside?	¿Hay mascotas adentro?	eye mask-**CO**-tas ah-**DEN**-tro
Cats or dogs	Gatos o perros	**GA**-toes oh **PAY**-rows
Do you have a problem with the smoke?	¿Tiene problemas con el humo?	t-**N**-a pro-**BLAY**-mas con el **OO**-mo
Do you need an ambulance?	¿Necesita una ambulancia?	nay-say-see-**TA** oon am-boo-**LAN**-see-ah
I need a witness.	Necesito un testigo.	nay-say-**SEE**-toe oon test-**TEE**-go
Lie down.	Acuéstese	ah-coo-**A**-stay-say
Calm down	Cálmese	**CAL**-may-say
Were you drinking?	¿Estaba tomando?	ace-**TA**-baa to-**MAN**-doe
Were you unconscious?	¿Estaba inconsciente?	ace-**TA**-baa in-con-see-**N**-tay
Don't move.	No se mueva	no say moo-**A**-va
Everything is OK.	Todo está bien.	**TO**-do ace-**TA** B-N
Don't worry.	No se preocupe.	no say pray-oh-**COO**-pay
I am going to help you.	Voy a ayudarle.	voy ah eye-you-**DAR**-lay
Do you have a smoke detector?	Tiene un detector de humo.	t-**N**-a oon day-tec-**TOR** day **OO**-mo

Tips & Techniques

Between 1995 and 2000, foreign-born Mexican workers accounted for more than two thirds (69%) of the 2,440 work-related fatalities.

In An Emergency — En Un Emergencia

No matter what language we speak, most of us are terrified in an emergency. When you are involved in situations involving Latin Americans, their fear is going to be caused by three distinctly different factors. First, they are just as scared of the fire as anyone else would be. Next, if they are not legal residents, they may be afraid of you and your uniform. Many Hispanics are quite fearful of professionals wearing uniforms. Things are very different in other parts of the world. They may also worry that you will turn them over to immigration for deportation. Lastly, because many Latin Americans distrust banks, they may have their entire savings tucked away under a mattress. Learn and practice the following phrases so you'll know what to say in an *emergencia.*

English	Español	Guide
Are there people in	Hay personas en	eye pear-**SOWN**-nas in
Are there children in	Hay niños en	eye **KEEN**-yos in
Are there pets in	Hay animales en	eye ah-knee-**MAL**-ace in
	Hay mascotas en	eye mask-**CO**-tas in
The house	Casa	**CA**-sa
The building	Edificio	a-dee-**FEE**-see-oh
The car	Carro	**CAR**-row
	Coche	**CO**-chay
The truck	Trucka	**TRUCK**-ah
	Camión	ca-me-**ON**
On the boat	En el bote	in el **BOW**-tay
Where	¿Dónde?	**DON**-day
How many	¿Cuántos?	coo-**AN**-toes
What floor?	¿En qué piso?	in kay **PEE**-so

English	Español	Guide
Who is inside	¿Quién está en el interior?	key-**N** ace-**TA** in el in-tay-ree-**OR**
Your baby	Su bebé	sue bay-**BAY**
Your child	Su niño	sue **KEEN**-yo
Your wife	Su esposa	sue ace-**PO**-sa
Your husband	Su esposo	sue ace-**PO**-so
Your friend	Su amigo	sue ah-**ME**-go
Your grandmother	Su abuela	sue ah-boo-**A**-la
Your grandfather	Su abuelo	sue ah-boo-**A**-low
What's your baby's name?	¿Cómo se llama su bebé?	**CO**-mo say **YA**-ma sue bay-**BAY**
What's your child's name?	¿Cómo se llama su niño?	**CO**-mo say **YA**-ma sue **KNEEN**-yo
What's your wife's name	¿Cómo se llama su esposa?	**CO**-mo say **YA**-ma sue ace-**PO**-sa
Where is the fire?	¿Dónde está el fuego?	**DON**-day ace-**TA** el foo-**A**-go
Are you OK?	¿Está bien?	ace-**TA** bN
Were you burned?	¿Se quemó?	say kay-**MO**
By fire	Por el fuego	pour el foo-**A**-go
By gasoline	Por la gasolina	pour la gas-oh-**LEAN**-na
By steam	Por el vapor	pour el vah-**POUR**
By chemicals	Por los químicos	pour los **KEY**-me-cos
Danger!	¡Peligro	pay-**LEE**-grow
It's dangerous!	¡Es peligroso!	es pay-lee-**GROW**-so

Orders and Commands — Órdenes y Mandatos

The beauty of language is that there are usually so many different ways to say the same thing. As long as you get your idea across, none of them is wrong! After all, the whole purpose of giving a command is to get someone to pay attention to you quickly. This important part of communication gives you several options. Some are quite simple and don't involve new vocabulary!

The first area to consider is body language. Always use as many direct motions with your hands and arms as possible. According to communication theory, people tend to understand gestures faster than spoken words. That's because no interpretation is needed. You see the signal and automatically understand. When words are used, you have to hear them, process them, and then act.

Secondly, consider the simple word *no*. Any time you need to make a command negative in Spanish, just start with *no*. There's no need to do anything else.

Next, the Spanish language is infused with courtesy. If all that comes to your mind is the required verb or action word, follow it with *por favor*. Another option is to start your sentence with *favor de* followed by the verb. This construction is grammatically perfect, and people will be impressed with your respect for their language.

English	Español	Guide
Be careful.	Cuidado	kwee-**DA**-doe
Breathe deeply	Respire profundo	ray-**SPEAR**-ray pro-**FOON**-doe
Breathe normally.	Respire normal.	ray-**SPEAR**-ray nor-**MAL**

English	Español	Guide
Call an ambulance.	Llame la ambulancia.	**YA**-may la am-boo-**LAN**-see-ah
Calm down.	Cálmese	**CAL**-may-say
Climb down the ladder.	Baje por la escalera.	**BA**-hey pour la ace-ca-**LAY**-ra
Close the door.	Cierre la puerta.	see-**A**-ray la poo-**AIR**-ta
Come here.	Venga aquí.	**VEN**-ga ah-**KEY**
Come with me.	Venga con migo	**VEN**-ga con **ME**-go
Cover	Cubra	**COO**-bra
Crawl	Gatee	**GA**-tay-a
Don't jump.	No salte	no **SALT**-tay
Don't move.	No se mueva.	no say moo-**A**-va
Don't open the door.	No abra la puerta.	no **AH**-bra la poo-**AIR**-ta
Don't stand up.	No se levante.	no se lay-**VAN**-tay
Don't use the elevator.	No use el ascensor.	no **OO**-say el ah-sen-**SOAR**
Use the stairs.	Use las escaleras.	**OO**-say las ace-ca-**LAIR**-ray
Don't worry	No se preocupe.	no say pray-**OH**-coo-pay
Everything is OK.	Todo está bien.	**TOE**-doe ace-**TA** bN
Explain	Explique	x-**PLEE**-kay
Get away.	Aléjese	ah-**LAY**-hey say
Get out	Salga	**SAL**-ga
Grab my hand.	Agarre mi mano.	ah-**GA**-ray me **MA**-no
Help	Socorro	so-**CORE**-oh

English	Español	Guide
Help me	Ayúdeme	eye-**YOU**-day-may
Hurry	Apúrese	ah-**POO**-ray-say
Lift	Levante	lay-**VAN**-tay
Look for	Busque	**BOOSE**-kay
Leave now	Váyase ahora	**VA**-ya-say ah-**OR**-ra
Lie down	Acuéstese	ah-coo-**ACE**-tay-say
Now	Ahora	ah-**OR**-ra
Quick	Rápido	**RA**-pee-doe
Relax	Relájese	ray-**LA**-hey-say
Rest	Descanse	des-**CAN**-say
Sit down	Siéntese	see-**N**-tay-say
Squeeze my hand	Apriete mi mano	ah-pre-**A**-tay me **MA**-no

Tips and Tidbits

A six-year, federally funded project that studied the health and life span of Latinos in the United States suggested that Latinos have longer life spans than other groups, despite having less access to healthcare and higher poverty rates. The research study followed 16,000 Latinos including Mexicans, Cubans, Puerto Ricans and individuals of central and South American origin.

People in the Hospital
Personas en el hospital

In an emergency, you could find yourself working in a hospital environment. While there, you might run into a visitor or a patient who will ask you about members of the hospital staff. This vocabulary list contains important members of the medical team. Since so many of the words are similar to their English equivalents, the list is relatively easy to learn.

Work steadily to improve your Spanish skills. The key to fluency is practice! Remember the story about the race between the tortoise and the hare? The tortoise kept a slow, steady pace and finished the race, while the rabbit burned himself out by going too fast. Attempt one word or phrase each day. Keep sticky notes and a pen in your car. Place one new word or phrase on the steering wheel of your car first thing every morning. Every time you stop, take a look at the word of the day. Try to use this word in a conversation throughout the day. By maintaining a slow steady pace, you will be able to dramatically increase your vocabulary in a few short months.

English	Español	Guide
Assistant	Ayudante	ay-oo-**DAN**-tay
Doctor	Doctor	doc-**TOR**
	Doctora	doc-**TOR**-rah
In-patient	Paciente interno	pa-see-**N**-tay n-**TER**-no
Nurse	Enfermera *(o)*	n-fair-**MARE**-rah
Out-patient	Paciente externo	pa-see-**N**-tay x-**TER**-no
Paramedic	Paramédico *(a)*	para-**MAY**-d-co
Patient	Paciente	pa-see-**N**-tay

English	Español	Guide
Pharmacist	Farmacéutico *(a)*	far-ma-**SAY**-oo-t-co
Police	Policía	poe-lee-**SEE**-ah
Receptionist	Recepcionista	ray-cept-see-on-**KNEES**-ta
Secretary	Secretaria	sec-ree-**TAR**-ree-ah
Security guard	Guardia de seguridad	goo-**ARE**-dee-ah day say-goo-ree-**DAD**
Supervisor	Supervisor *(a)*	soo-pear-**V**-soar
Therapist	Terapeuta	terra-pay-**OO**-ta
Visitor	Visitante	v-see-**TAN**-tay

Places in the Hospital — Lugares en el Hospital

As a first responder, people look up to you and expect you to know who everyone is and where everything is located. Knowing how to give directions to places in the hospital will be an important skill for you. The following is a list of hospital departments or *departamentos*. Notice that many of the terms for the hospital's departments *en español* are similar to those in English. Here's an important tip: Always remember to say the full name of the department rather than using letter abbreviations such as ER and ICU. People who are new to speaking English won't know what these letters signify!

English	Español	Guide
Basement	Sótano	**SO**-tan-oh
Cafeteria	Cafetería	ca-fay-ter-**REE**-ah
Department	Departamento	day-par-ta-**MEN**-toe

English	Español	Guide
Elevator	Ascensor	ah-sen-**SOAR**
Emergency room	Sala de emergencia	**SAL**-la day a-mare-**HEN**-see ah
Entrance	Entrada	in-**TRA**-dah
Exit	Salida	sal-**LEE**-da
Gift shop	Tienda de regalos	t-**N**-da day ray-**GAL**-os
Hall	Corredor	core-ray-**DOOR**
Intensive care	Cuidados intensivos	kwe-**DA**-does n-ten-**SEE**-vows
Laboratory	Laboratorio	lab-oh-rah-**TOR**-e-oh
Lobby	Salón	sal-**ON**
Maternity	Maternidad	ma-ter-knee-**DAD**
Operating room	Sala de operaciones	**SAL**-la day oh-pear-rah-see-**ON**-ace
Parking lot	Estacionamiento	es-ta-see-on-ah-me-**N**-toe
Pediatrics	Pediátrico	pay-d-**AH**-tree-co
Physical therapy	Terapia física	ter-**RAH**-p-ah **FEE**-see-ka
Radiology	Radiología	rah-d-oh-low-**HE**-ah
Recovery room	Sala de recuperación	**SAL**-la day ray-coo-pear-ra-see-**ON**
Respiratory therapy	Terapia respiratoria	ter-**RAH**-p-ah res-pier-ah-**TOR**-e-ah
Rest rooms	Sanitarios Baño	san-knee-**TAR**-ree-ohs **BAN**-yo
Stairs	Escaleras	es-ka-**LAIR**-as
Telephone	Teléfono	tay-**LAY**-fono

English	Español	Guide
Waiting room	Sala de espera	SAL-la day es-PEAR-ah
Water fountain	Fuente de agua	foo-N-tay day AH-gua
X-ray	Rayos equis	rah-yos A-kees

Please Call a Doctor!
¡Favor de llamar a un doctor!

When you are called upon to evaluate a patient's illness or injury, quick reactions and good communication are essential to handling the crisis. Your knowledge of the basic parts of human anatomy will give you and your patient confidence. Knowing these terms will also help you build trust with your patient and other family members. Communicating with everyone on the scene is *muy importante*.

Listed below are laymen's terms for the various parts of the body. Because you will be dealing with Hispanics from all parts of the Spanish-speaking world, this list will help you communicate quickly with all of them. Learning these parts of the body will help you in any emergency situation — they may even help you save a life!

English	Español	Guide
Ankle	Tobillo	toe-B-yo
Arm	Brazo	BRA-so
Back	Espalda	ace-PALL-doe da
Body	Cuerpo	coo-AIR-poe

English	Español	Guide
Brain	Cerebro	say-**RAY**-bro
Chest	Pecho	**PAY**-cho
Chin	Barbilla	bar-**B**-ya
Ear	Oreja	oh-**RAY**-ha
Eye	Ojo	**OH**-ho
Face	Cara	**CA**-ra
Finger	Dedo	**DAY**-do
Foot	Pie	**P**-ay
Hand	Mano	**MA**-no
Head	Cabeza	ca-**BAY**-sa
Heart	Corazón	core-ra-**SEWN**
Knee	Rodilla	row-**D**-ya
Leg	Pierna	p-**YAIR**-na
Mouth	Boca	**BOW**-ca
Nail	Uña	**OON**-ya
Neck	Cuello	coo-**A**-yo
Nose	Nariz	na-**REECE**
Skin	Piel	p-**L**
Shoulder	Hombro	**ON**-bro
Spine	Espina	ace-**P**-na
Stomach	Estómago	ace-**TOE**-ma-go
Throat	Garganta	gar-**GAN**-ta
Toe	Dedo del pie	**DAY**-doe del **P**-a
Tooth	Diente	d-**N**-tay
Wrist	Muñeca	moon-**YEA**-ca

The Body — El Cuerpo

Eye — Ojo

Temple — Sien

Hand — Mano

Wrist — Muñeca

Arm — Brazo

Finger — Dedo

Neck — Cuello

Shoulder — Hombro

Abdomen — Abdomen
Stomach — Estómago

Chest
Pecho

Leg
Pierna

Back
Espalda

Buttocks
Nalgas

Groin — Ingle

Heel — Talón

Foot — Pie

Toe — Dedo del pie

The Face — La Cara

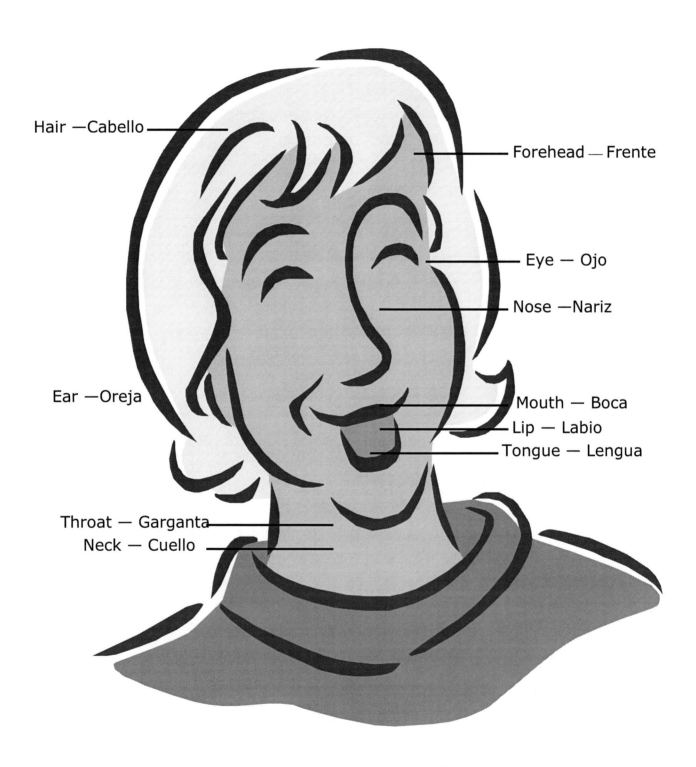

Hair —Cabello

Forehead — Frente

Eye — Ojo

Nose —Nariz

Ear —Oreja

Mouth — Boca

Lip — Labio

Tongue — Lengua

Throat — Garganta

Neck — Cuello

The Internal Organs — Los Órganos Internos

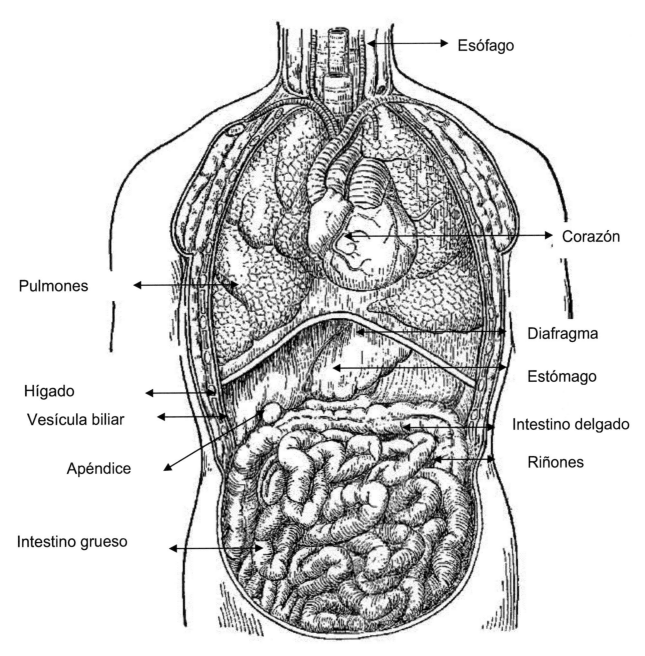

Esófago

Corazón

Pulmones

Diafragma

Estómago

Hígado

Vesícula biliar

Intestino delgado

Apéndice

Riñones

Intestino grueso

Recto, Colon, Ano

Are You in Pain? — ¿Tiene Dolor?

A few years ago, I was honored by being invited to attend the birth of a friend's child. Carmen, who grew up in Puerto Rico, is completely bilingual, but Spanish is her first language. She has achieved amazing fluidity in her speech and she never stumbles in either language. Watching the miracle of birth was amazing, but hearing the effect the physical discomfort had on Carmen's ability to speak English was even *more* eye-opening. The more pain Carmen endured, the more difficulty she had speaking and translating English. As the baby's head appeared, each of the three nurses who were present said something different in English. "Push!" "She's almost here!" "It won't be long now!"

At the same time, the doctor was attempting to explain to Carmen what was happening. Her sister was also in the room and she was speaking to Carmen in Spanish. Her husband was also there trying to comfort her in English. It was a cacophony of noise! When she finally had enough, Carmen shouted, "Shut up! I need to hear the doctor. The rest of you just please shut up. Spanish is still my first language." When the pain increased, thinking in both languages was just too much for her.

That's when it hit me. *Even under the best conditions, speaking a foreign language can be a challenge. However, when intense physical discomfort is added, the level of difficulty increases exponentially.* Pain pushes the body to its limits. Every nerve ending ends up working over-time. Even if individuals are bilingual, you must take this fact into consideration when working with Spanish-speaking patients. Because of the physical discomfort they are suffering, you must allow them more time to translate from English to Spanish. They are also going to have more difficulty remembering English words, *even if they have been speaking English their entire life.*

When a Spanish-speaking patient discusses pain and discomfort, the concepts are expressed differently than in English. Rather than *being* in pain, you *have* pain *en español*. Refer to the chapter on irregular verbs for more uses of the word *tener*. Frequently, you will hear the words ***tengo dolor*** which means ***I have*** pain. This phrase is followed by the word for the affected area. When you are asking if the patient is in pain, use the phrase *¿tiene dolor?*

Were you
Estaba

In the
front
↓
en frente

In back
↓
detrás

Alone
↓
Solo

English	Español	Guide
Does it hurt?	¿Le duele?	lay do-A-lay
Where?	¿Dónde?	DON-day
Show me.	Indícalo.	een-D-ca-low
It hurts.	Me duele.	may do-A-lay
Do you have pain?	¿Tiene dolor?	t-N-a doe-LORE
Do you have a lot of pain?	¿Tiene mucho dolor?	t-N-a MOO-cho doe-LORE
Is the pain mild?	¿Tiene dolor moderado?	t-N-a doe-LORE mo-dare-RAH-doe
Is the pain intermittent?	¿Tiene dolor intermitente?	t-N-a doe-LORE n-ter-me-TENT-tay
Is the pain deep?	¿Tiene dolor profundo?	t-N-a doe-LORE pro-FOON-doe
Is the pain constant?	¿Tiene dolor constante?	t-N-a doe-LORE con-STAN-tay
Is the pain burning?	¿Tiene dolor quemante?	t-N-a doe-LORE kay-MAN-tay
Is the pain severe?	¿Tiene dolor muy fuerte?	t-N-a doe-LORE foo-AIR-tay
Is the pain throbbing?	¿Tiene dolor pulsante?	t-N-a doe-LORE pull-SAN-tay
Using the numbers from one through ten indicate the level of your pain.	Usando los números de uno hasta diez, indique el nivel de su dolor.	oo-SAND-doe los NEW-may-rows day OO-no AH-sta d-ACE n-D-kay l knee-VEL day su do-LORE

107

Diseases — Enfermedades

In this list of common diseases, the strong relationship between our two languages is *obvio*, isn't it? Did you notice that the Spanish word *"enfermedad"*

looks a lot like the English word "infirmity"? Sí, both words have Latin origins. It won't take you long to get the hang of this. Here's a tip to help you get started. Diseases in English that end in the suffix *"-itis"* such as arthritis, bursitis and tendonitis are essentially the same words in Spanish. If the words aren't identical, try using the Latin root from your medical studies. That's usually a good place to start.

English	Español	Guide
Anemia	Anemia	ah-**NAY**-me-ah
Appendicitis	Apendicitis	ah-pen-d-**SEE**-tees
Arthritis	Artritis	are-**TREE**-tees
Asthma	Asma	**AS**-ma
Bronchitis	Bronquitis	bron-**KEY**-tees
Cancer	Cáncer	**KAHN**-cer
Chicken pox	Varicela	va-ree-**SAY**-la
Cold	Catarro	ca-**TAR**-row
Diabetes	Diabetes	d-ah-**BAY**-tes
Fever	Fiebre	fee-**A**-bray
Flu	Influenza	n-flew-**N**-sa
Gall stones	Cálculos en la vesícula	**CAL**-coo-lows n la vay-**SEE**-coo-la
Glaucoma	Glaucoma	gl-ow-**CO**-ma
Hay fever	Fiebre de heno	fee-**A**-bray day **A**-no
Hepatitis	Hepatitis	ape-ah-**T**-tis

English	Español	Guide
Herpes	Herpes	**AIR**-pays
Hives	Urticaria	oor-t-**CA**-ree-ah
Hypoglycemia	Hipoglucemia	ee-po-glue-**SAY**-me-ah
Indigestion	Indigestión	n-dee-hess-t-**ON**
Jaundice	Ictericia	ick-tay-**REE**-see-ah
Kidney stones	Cálculos en los riñones	**CAL**-coo-lows n los reen-**NYO**-nays
Laryngitis	Laringitis	la-reen-**HE**-tees
Leukemia	Leucemia	lay-oo-**SAY**-me-ah
Measles	Sarampión	sa-ram-pee-**ON**
Mononucleosis	Mononucleosis	mo-no-new-clay-**OH**-sis
Mumps	Paperas	pa-**PEAR**-rahs
Pneumonia	Pulmonía	pool-mo-**KNEE**-ah
	Neumonía	nay-oo-mon-**KNEE**-ah
Tuberculosis	Tuberculosis	too-bear-coo-**LOW**-sis

More Common Problems

English	Español	Guide
Abscess	Absceso	ab-**SAY**-so
Blister	Ampolla	am-**PO**-ya
Broken bone	Hueso roto	who-**AY**-so **ROW**-toe
	Fractura	frac-**TOO**-rah

English	Español	Guide
Bruise	Contusión	con-too-see-**ON**
Bump	Hinchazón	eem-cha-**SEWN**
Burn	Quemadura	kay-ma-**DO**-ra
Chills	Escalofrío	es-ca-low-**FREE**-oh
Cough	Tos	toes
Cramps	Calambre	ca-**LAMB**-bray
Diarrhea	Diarrea	dee-ah-**RAY**-ah
Fever	Fiebre	fee-**A**-bray
Migraine	Jaqueca	ja-**KAY**-ca
	Migraña	me-**GRAN**-ya
Rash	Erupción	a-roop-see-**ON**
Sprain	Torcedura	tor-say-**DO**-ra
Swelling	Inflamación	een-fla-ma-see-**ON**
Wound	Herido	a-**REE**-doe

Useful Assessment Questions

¿Tiene diabetes?   Do you have diabetes?

¿Tiene asma?   Do you have asthma?

¿Está embarazada?   Are you pregnant?

¿Tiene náusea?   Are you nauseous?

¿Tiene problemas con su corazón?   Do you have heart problems?

¿Qué medicinas toma?   What medicines are you taking?

¿Es usted débil?   Are you weak?

¿Qué día es hoy?   What day is it?

¿Cómo se siente?   How do you feel?

¿Tiene dolor de cuello?   Do you have neck pain?

¿Tiene dolor de espalda?   Do you have back pain?

¿Tiene dolor de pecho?   Do you have chest pain?

Remedies and Medicines
Remedios y Medicinas

You are going to be pleasantly surprised when you see all the English-Spanish matches or *cognates* in the following list of remedies and medicines. These really are your *amigos*! Since many drugs or *drogas* are invented in the US, the name of a medicine is often derived from Latin. This gives our vocabulary substantial common ground. Even product names are good to try. Common brand names are not translated into Spanish. *El Tylenol* is, after all, a global product!

English	Español	Guide
Tablet	Tableta	ta-**BLAY**-ta
Capsule	Cápsula	**CAP**-soo-la
Pill	Píldora	**PEEL**-dor-ah
Lozenge	Pastilla	pahs-**T**-ya
Analgesic	Analgésico	ah-nal-**HEY**-see-co
Anesthetic	Anestésico	ah-nay-**STAY**-see-co
Antacid	Antiácido	ahn-t-**AH**-see-doe
Antibiotic	Antibiótico	ahn-t-b-**OH**-t-co
Anticoagulant	Anticoagulante	ahn-t-co-ah-goo-**LAN**-tay
Antidote	Antídoto	ahn-**T**-oh-doe
Antihistamine	Antihistamínicos	ahn-t-ees-ta-**MEAN**-knee-cos
Anti-inflammatory	Anti-inflamatorio	ahn-t-een-fla-ma-**TOR**-ree-oh
Antiseptic	Antiséptico	ahn-t-**SEP**-t-co
Aspirin	Aspirina	ahs-p-**REE**-na

English	Español	Guide
Barbiturate	Barbitúrico	bar-b-**TOO**-ree-co
Chemotherapy	Quimioterapia	key-me-oh-ter-**RA**-p-ah
Codeine	Codeína	co-day-**EE**-na
Contraceptive	Contraceptivo	con-tra-cep-**T**-vo
Cough drop	Pastillas para la tos	pas-**T**-yas **PA**-ra la toes
Cough syrup	Jarabe para la tos	ha-**RA**-bay **PA**-ra la toes
Cortisone	Cortisona	core-tee-**SO**-na
Cream	Crema	**CRAY**-ma
Diuretic	Diurético	d-oo-**RAY**-t-co
Inhaler	Inhalador	n-ah-la-**DOOR**
Insulin	Insulina	n-soo-**LEAN**-ah
Laxative	Laxante	lax-**AN**-tay
Lotion	Loción	lo-see-**ON**
Morphine	Morfina	more-**FEE**-na
Narcotic	Narcótico	nar-**CO**-t-co
Nitroglycerine	Nitroglicerina	knee-tro-glee-ser-**REE**-na
Nutritional supplement	Suplemento nutricional	sou-play-**MEN**-toe new-tree-see-on-**NAL**
Penicillin	Penicilina	pay-knee-see-**LEE**-na
Sedative	Sedante	say-**DAN**-tay
Steroid	Esteroide	es-stair-**ROY**-day
Suppositories	Supositorios	sue-po-see-**TOR**-ree-ohs
Tranquilizers	Tranquilizantes	tran-key-lee-**SAN**-tays

Side Effects — Efectos Adversos

As you work with your patient, your next step will be to discuss possible side effects of any medication they are taking. This could have a bearing on the symptoms you witness.

Regardless of what language you speak, side effects are never pleasant. In *español* there are several ways to address the term "side effects." You can be quite literal and call them bad or adverse effects like the title of this section demonstrates. In addition, the phrase "bad reaction" or *mala reacción* is also used.

English	Español	Guide
Allergies	Alergias	ah-**LAIR**-he-ahs
Anxiety	Ansiedad	an-see-a-**DAD**
Bad reaction	Mala reacción	**MAL**-ah ray-ax-see-**ON**
Bleeding	Sangrado	san-**GRA**-doe
Constipation	Estreñimiento	es-train-knee-me-**N**-toe
Cramps	Calambres	ca-**LAMB**-rays
Decrease of appetite	Disminución del apetito	dis-me-new-see-**ON** del ah-pay-**T**-toe
Dizziness	Mareos	ma-**RAY**-ohs
	Vértigo	**VER**-t-go
Dry mouth	Boca seca	**BOW**-ca **SAY**-ca
Headache	Dolor de cabeza	doe-**LORE** day ca-**BAY**-sa
High blood pressure	Presión alta	pray-see-**ON AL**-ta

English	Español	Guide
Hives	Ronchas de la piel	**RON**-chas day la p-**L**
Increase of appetite	Aumento del apetito	ow-**MEN**-toe del ah-pay-**T**-toe
Insomnia	Insomnio	n-**SOM**-knee-oh
Itching	Picazón	p-ca-**SEWN**
Low blood pressure	Presión baja	pray-see-**ON BAA**-ha
Rash	Erupción	a-rupt-see-**ON**
Sleepiness	Sueño	sue-**AY**-nyo
Tremor	Temblor	tem-**BLORE**
Weight gain	Aumento de peso	ow-**MEN**-toe day **PAY**-so

Tips & Techniques

According to the US Department of Health and Human Services:

1. The health of Latina women varies between sub-groups. Mexican-American women tend to have lower rates of high blood pressure than both African-American and Caucasian women.

2. Hispanic women experience the highest rates of cervical cancer and the second highest death rates from cervical cancer in the US.

3. The leading causes of death for Hispanic women are heart disease, cancer, stroke and diabetes.

4. Arthritis is the second most common chronic disease found in Hispanic women, and the second leading cause of activity limitation.

5. Cancer is the second leading cause of death in Hispanic women.

6. Breast cancer diagnoses are increasing among Hispanic women.

7. More than 25% of Hispanic women aged 65-74 have Type II diabetes.

Are you Pregnant? — ¿Está embarazada?

Hispanic women, especially those who have recently immigrated to America, face many more challenges in accessing healthcare than other minority women. The more acculturated a woman is, the greater her access to health care services. Working with Latin American women requires a delicate approach. This is especially true with women over the age of 30. Older Latina women tend to be extremely shy and inhibited about personal health issues. Therefore, establishing a rapport with them is especially critical. Use this vocabulary list to help you in the assessment of pregnancy issues.

English	Español	Guide
Are you pregnant?	¿Está embarazada	es-**TA** m-ba-ra-**SA**-da
How many months?	¿Cuántos meses?	coo-**WAN**-toes **MAY**-ses
Weeks	Semanas	**SAY**-ma-**NAS**
Bleeding	Hemorragia	san-gra-me-**N**-toe
Discharge	Flujo	**FLEW**-ho
Labor pains	Dolores de parto	do-**LORE**-ace day **PAR**-toe
Your period	Su regla	sue **RAY**-gla
	Su menstruación	sue men-strew-ah-see-**ON**
Sexually transmitted disease	Enfermedad transmitida por relaciones	n-fer-me-**DAD** trans-me-**TEE**-da por ray-la-see-**ON**-ace
Natural childbirth	Parto natural	**PAR**-toe na-too-**RAL**
Rectal exam	Examen del recto	x-**AH**-men del **WRECK**-toe

Giving Instructions

Giving instructions in a gentle but authoritative way will help you in almost any situation. Review the following list. Highlight the phrases you will use most often and learn them first.

English	Español	Guide
Sit down	Siéntese	see-**N**-tay-say
Sit on the chair.	Siéntese en la silla.	see-**N**-tay-say n la **SEE**-ya
Stand up	Levántese	lay-**VAN**-tay-say
Breathe deeply.	Respire profundo.	ray-**SPEE**-ray pro-**FOON**-doe
Take a deep breath.	Aspire profundo.	ahs-**PIER**-ray pro-**FOON**-doe
Open your mouth.	Abre la boca.	**AH**-bray la **BOW**-ca
Get undressed.	Desvístase	days-**VEES**-ta-say
Lie down.	Acuéstese.	ah-coo-**ACE**-tay-say
Turn around.	Voltéese	vol-**TAY**-a-say
Wait	Espérese	es-**PAY**-ray-say
Wait here.	Espérese aquí.	es-**PAY**-ray-say ah-**KEY**
Come here	Venga aquí.	**VEN**-ga ah-**KEY**
Get up	Súbase	**SOO**-ba-say
Get up on the table	Súbase a la mesa.	**SOO**-ba-say ah la **MAY**-sa
Sign your name.	Firme su nombre.	**FEAR**-may sue **NOM**-bray
Sign here	Firme aquí	**FEAR**-may ah-**KEY**
Calm down	Cálmese	**CAL**-may-say

Calming Patients — Calmando Pacientes

Good customer service involves building a good relationship with Latino patients. The path to starting this relationship often begins with a smile and a simple phrase or two. On the following list, you will find some great "one-liners" that will help you get started. Talking to parents about their children is a great way to begin. Everyone wants to talk about their children. Practice these often and have fun! You will receive lots of smiles and encouragement!

English	Español	Guide
Don't worry.	No se preocupe.	no say pray-oh-**COO**-pay
Good luck!	¡Buena suerte!	boo-**WAY**-na **SWEAR**-tay
Calm down!	¡Cálmese!	**CAL**-may-say
How pretty!	¡Qué bonito! (m) ¡Qué bonita! (f) ¡Qué lindo! (m) ¡Qué linda! (f)	kay bow-**KNEE**-toe kay bow-**KNEE**-ta kay **LEAN**-doe kay **LEAN**-da
He's precious! She's precious!	¡Es precioso! ¡Es preciosa!	ace pray-see-**OH**-so ace pray-see-**OH**-sa
What a smile!	¡Qué sonrisa!	kay son-**REE**-sa
Have a nice day!	¡Qué le vaya bien! Tenga un buen día.	kay lay **VA**-ya b-N **TEN**-ga oon boo-**WAYNE DEE**-ah
How old is your baby?	¿Cuántos años tiene su bebé?	coo-**AN**-toes **AN**-yos t-N-a sue bay-**BAY**
What's your baby's name?	¿Cómo se llama su bebé?	**CO**-mo say **YA**-ma sue bay-**BAY**

Diabetes and Latinos

According to the American Diabetes Association, diabetes in the US Hispanic population has reached epidemic proportions. Within this diverse ethnic group, diabetes is two to three times more common in Mexican American and Puerto Rican adults than in Central American Hispanics or Cubans. Many go undiagnosed because Hispanics have a lower than average level of preventative healthcare. It's possible that as many as 675,000 Hispanic Americans have diabetes and do not even realize it. Many studies find that almost every Latino knows at least one other Latino who is affected by this disease.

Common Symptoms of Diabetes

English	Español	Guide
Chronic fatigue	Cansancio crónico	cahn-**SAHN**-see-oh **CROW**-knee-co
Thirst	Sed	said
Frequent urination	Orina con frecuencia	or-**REE**-na con fray-coo-**N**-see-ah
Blurred vision	Visión borrosa	v-see-**ON** bow-**ROW**-sa
Sudden weight loss	Pérdida súbita de peso	**PEAR**-d-da **SUE**-b-ta day **PAY**-so
Wounds that won't heal	Heridas que no sanan	air-**REE**-das kay no **SA**-nan
Vaginal infections	Infecciones vaginales	een-fec-see-**ON**-ace va-he-**NAL**-ace
Numbness or tingling in the hands or feet	Adormecimiento u hormigueo en las manos o pies	ah-door-may-see-me-**N**-toe oo or-me-**GWAY**-nay-oh in las **MA**-nose oh p-**ACE**

Typing in Spanish on Your Computer

When you need to type documents containing accent marks or Spanish punctuation, you will use keys that you have probably never used before. Actually, you are *composing characters* using the **control** key. This key is located on the bottom row of your keyboard. This is such an important key that you will see it on both sides of the keyboard. This key prevents the computer from moving forward one space so the accent is placed on *top* of the letter instead of *beside* it.

Always remember to hold the control key down first. With a little practice, this will become a normal part of your keyboarding skills.

If you are using MS Word, you may also use the menu command *Insert>Symbol*.

To insert	For a PC, Press	For a Mac, Press
á, é, í, ó, ú, ý Á, É, Í, Ó, Ú, Ý	CTRL+' (APOSTROPHE), *the letter*	OPTION + e, *the letter*
â, ê, î, ô, û Â, Ê, Î, Ô, Û	CTRL+SHIFT+^ *the letter*	OPTION + i, *the letter*
ã, ñ, õ Ã, Ñ, Õ	CTRL+SHIFT+~ (TILDE), *the letter*	OPTION + n, *the letter*
ä, ë, ï, ö, ü, ÿ Ä, Ë, Ï, Ö, Ü, Ÿ	CTRL+SHIFT+: (COLON), *the letter*	OPTION + u, *the letter*
¿	ALT+CTRL+SHIFT+?	OPTION+SHIFT+ ?
¡	ALT+CTRL+SHIFT+!	OPTION + !

Basic Information
Please print

Date: _____
              Month   Day   Year

Mr.
Mrs.
Miss_____
      First Name   *Middle Name*   *Paternal Surname*   *Maternal Surname (Husband)*

Address:_____
                                  Street

_____
City   *State*   *Zip Code*

Telephone: **Home**_____   **Work**_____

             Cell_____   **Fax** _____

Email Address: _____

Social Security Number: _____-_____-_____

Date of birth   _____
                     Month   Day   Year

Driver's License Number: _____

Occupation: _____

Place of employment: _____

Marital Status: ☐   Married
                ☐   Single
                ☐   Divorced
                ☐   Separated
                ☐   Widow

Husband's name:_____
                 First Name   *Middle Name*   *Paternal Surname* *Maternal Surname (Husband)*
Wife's name: _____
                 First Name   *Middle Name*   *Paternal Surname Maternal Surname (Husband)*

In case of emergency: _____ **Telephone:** _____

Signature: _____ **Date:** _____

Practicing What You Have Learned

Practice is an important part of the language learning process. The more you include practice in your daily routine, the more comfortable and fluent you will become. There is no easy way to practice. It just takes time. The key to practicing Spanish is to set realistic goals. Don't let the language learning process overwhelm you. Yes, there is a lot to learn, and it will take some time. However, by setting realistic goals, you have a greater chance of sticking with it. Since each of us has a different learning style, find out what works best for you and break the material down into small pieces. Some of us learn best by listening. Others need to write the words and phrases in order to visualize them. Generally, the more of your senses that you involve in the learning process, the faster you will retain the information. Therefore, focus and practice one thing at a time. Doing little things will make the greatest difference in the long run. Working five minutes every day on your Spanish is *mucho* better than trying to incorporate an hour of practice time only once each week. Consistency in your practice is critical.

Here are some practice tips that have worked for me and others who have participated in *SpeakEasy Spanish*™ training programs over the years.

1. Start practicing first thing in the morning. The shower is a great place to start. Say the numbers or run through the months of the year while you wash your hair. If you practice when you start your day, you are more likely to continue to practice as the day progresses.

2. Use your commute time to practice. Listening to CDs, music and Spanish language radio stations will help you learn the rhythm of Spanish. Your vocabulary will also increase.

3. If you are stopped in traffic, look around for numbers on billboards or the license plates of other cars to help you practice. As they say, don't just sit there — do something!

4. Investigate sites on the internet such as www.about.spanish.com and www.studyspanish.com. These are great places to practice and learn, not to mention the fact they are free!

5. Buy Spanish magazines or obtain Spanish newspapers that are published in your area. Many magazines such as *People* have Spanish versions and almost every community in the country has one or two Spanish language newspapers. Many of these are free.

6. If there are no Spanish newspapers available in your area, you can find a variety of publications from Latin America online. All the major cities in Latin America have newspapers that are easy to find online.

7. Practice as often as possible — even five minutes a day will help.

8. Don't give up! You didn't learn English overnight, and you won't learn Spanish that way either. Set realistic goals and don't go too far, too fast.

9. Learn five to ten words each week.

10. Practice at work with a friend.

11. Read! The following books will make great additions to your library:

Baez, Francia and Chong, Nilda. *Latino Culture.* Intercultural Press, 2005

Einsohn, Marc and Steil, Gail. *The Idiot's Guide to Learning Spanish on Your Own.* Alpha Books, 1996

Hawson, Steven R. *Learn Spanish the Lazy Way.* Alpha Books, 1999.

Reid, Elizabeth. Spanish *Lingo for the Savvy Gringo.* In One Ear Publications, 1997

Wald, Susana. *Spanish for Dummies.* Wiley Publishing, 2000.

About the Author

Myelita Melton, MA

Myelita Melton, founder of SpeakEasy Communications remembers the first time she heard a "foreign" language. She knew from that moment what she wanted to do with her life. "Since I was always the kid in class that talked too much," Myelita says, "I decided it would be a good idea to learn more than one language — that way I could talk to a lot more people!" After high school, she studied in Mexico at the *Instituto de Filológica Hispánica.* She completed both her BA and MA in French and Curriculum Design at Appalachian State University in Boone, NC. She has studied and speaks the following five languages: French, Spanish, Italian, German, and English.

"Lita's" unique career includes classroom instruction and challenging corporate experience. She has won several national awards, including a prestigious *Rockefeller* scholarship. In 1994, she was named in *Who's Who Among Outstanding Americans.* Myelita's corporate experience includes owning a television production firm, working with NBC's Spanish news division, *Canal de Noticias,* and Charlotte's PBS affiliate, WTVI. In her spare time, she continues to broadcast with WDAV, a National Public Radio affiliate near Lake Norman in North Carolina where she currently resides.

In 1997, Myelita started SpeakEasy Communications to offer industry specific Spanish instruction in North Carolina. The company is now the nation's leader in Spanish training, offering more than 30 *SpeakEasy Spanish*™ programs and publications to companies, associations, and colleges throughout the US.

MEMBER

NATIONAL SPEAKERS ASSOCIATION

Lita is also a member of the National Speaker's Association and the National Council for Continuing Education and Training. Many of her clients say she is the most high-energy, results-oriented speaker they have ever seen. As she travels the country speaking on languages and cultural diversity issues in the workplace, she is realizing her dream of being able to speak to the world!